THE HARDEST CLIMB

THE HARDEST CLIMB

BY ALISTAIR SUTCLIFFE

Bluemoose

Copyright © Alistair Sutcliffe 2011

First published in 2011 by
Bluemoose Books Ltd
25 Sackville Street
Hebden Bridge
West Yorkshire
HX7 7DJ

www.bluemoosebooks.com

British Library Cataloguing-in-Publication data
A catalogue record for this book is available from the-British-Library

Hardback   ISBN 13: 978-0-9566876-2-3

Printed and bound in the UK by Jellyfish Solutions Ltd

Foreword
by Sir Chris Bonington

It was 1975 when I first met Alistair at the home of the late Eric Major, who masterminded the production of my book, *Everest The Hard Way*, which tells the story of our ascent of the South West Face in September 1975. Alistair was a friend of his son and I had no idea of the impact that I had made on this young lad.

Now, 35 years later, he has his own remarkable story to tell. Alistair wrote his autobiography whilst recovering from a near-fatal brain haemorrhage. It describes his successful ascents of the highest mountain on each of the seven continents, and it is written with conviction and sensitivity. It details the beauty and perils of life high in the remote mountain ranges, describing intently both the joy of success and the heartache of tragedy that thwarts the self-indulgent world of high altitude climbing that some of us love so dearly.

Through his book, Alistair shares his experiences in graphic detail, compelling the reader to keep turning the pages. Success on all of the Seven Summits is a feat in itself, made all the more remarkable by the fact that they were all summited at the first attempt.

In Alistair's story, adventure, humanity and personal struggle combine to broaden the appeal to a wide readership.

The final chapter is especially moving. This truly is Alistair's hardest climb, and his recovery from the brain haemorrhage is extraordinary. All of the survival skills that a climber uses every day in the mountains have, undoubtedly, prepared Alistair for this, his greatest challenge. No-one ever knows what lies ahead of them in life, as this book demonstrates. His approach to his rehabilitation mimics the meticulous approach that he has to his climbs. His fund-raising efforts through the climbing expeditions and marathon running have helped touch the lives of many, and I'm sure that Saint Catherine's Hospice in Scarborough are very glad of his support.

November 2010

To Emily, Luke, Laurence
and Stefan

Prologue

February 1ˢᵗ 2010. Where the hell am I? I'm in a room, in a bed, my wife is crying, clutching my limp hand. There are doctors and nurses everywhere and leads coming from the skin on my chest. Tubes and needles are sticking out from both arms. I am in Intensive Care at Hull Royal Infirmary. I can't move...anything. Any limb that I try to contract, any ray of light that hits my pupils, any show of any emotion from my face- and the pain, God the pain. My head must not move from its current position. Any change sets the spiral off. First the vomiting, then the pain in my neck, rushing with spasms over the top of my head and into my eyes, a burning, visceral pain. It's serious. My mother and father are in the room. I can't open my eyes to see them, but I hear them there. I've suffered a catastrophic subarachnoid brain haemorrhage, and my 37-year-old wife has been told by the consultant in charge to expect the worst and say goodbye to me.

Slowly, very slowly, the gaps start to fill in. I had been at home, stepping into the bath. Suddenly my head felt as if it was going to explode. I'd stumbled downstairs to get my phone to call my wife at the hospital where she is a surgeon. I must have made the call, as I remember the dogs barking, confused and frightened, as an ambulance crew arrived at the house.

But something's wrong. I can't remember before that. Why? I don't know. I'm frightened. Will I ever walk again? Will I be able to see again? Will I die? I know the odds, they're not good. What has happened to my memory? These are my darkest hours. I piece bits together, and work out that I've lost six months of memory, from August 2009 up to the day of the haemorrhage, but everything else remains. The expeditions and adventures are in place. I remember back to when I was eleven years old....

Contents

Chapter 1
The Early Years and Mont Blanc

Our lives are measured by the footprints we leave behind, the courses we chart and the examples that we leave for others to follow.

I was eleven years old in 1975, the year that I met Chris Bonington. Chris was one of the worlds' foremost mountaineers and he'd just returned from leading the first successful British expedition to summit Mount Everest. Chris was visiting my best friend's father, Eric Major, himself a climber as well as a publisher. Paul and I had just come in from playing football on the local fields. On entering the familiar surroundings of Paul's house, I was greeted by an unfamiliar yet welcoming and friendly giant of a man. Standing tall in the kitchen, this strange man had a cracked, weather-beaten face covered by an uneven tan, with a thick untended beard, experienced eyes and a warm smile. This was Chris Bonington, and from the minute he started talking to me I was interested – quite something, for me. He recounted several stories of his trip, good *and* bad and that was me hooked. What does it really feel like to stand on top of the world? What would the air smell like up there? How can people get so high without being in a plane? What does it take to get up there, to the places where so few have been? 'One day', I thought to myself, 'I want to answer these questions'.

Life before secondary school had presented me with some indication of where my future might go. My father and I are similar in many ways, both sharing a love for animals and humans alike, though occasionally more for the former. In the late 1960s, before I was old enough to be trusted on my own at home in the school holidays, dad used to take me along to his surgery where I used to sit and play with my toys as he consulted with both ill and well patients. It was on one of his house visits, to an elderly patient who ran the local slaughter house, that I acquired my first real pet. As we stepped out of my father's old mini traveller, a lorry pulled up laden with chickens ready to be

1

"dressed" for the consumer. As the lorry driver threw the birds in through the slaughter-house door, I heard a loud "crack", and the bird that he had just thrown began squawking in obvious pain. The poor chicken had suffered a badly broken leg in the throwing process, and now lay shaking in distress on the stone floor. I must have been visibly upset at witnessing this cruelty, as dad stepped in without hesitation, and offered the slaughter-man's son three shillings and sixpence for the injured chicken. The offer was accepted, father went in to attend to his patient, and I attended to the stricken bird. That afternoon we got the chicken home and splinted its broken leg with two lollipop sticks and some bandage from the surgery. We named the pet Lazarus, as we felt that it had risen from its grave, and the chicken and I embarked on a nine year relationship together. I truly loved my pet, and doted on it to the extreme, regularly encouraging it in from the garden with pieces of chocolate and cream cracker, only to be shouted at by mother several hours later as she cleaned up the poo left behind by my new best friend. Lazzy never laid a single egg in her entire time with us, but she lived a very long and happy life in the Sutcliffe household, finally passing away after many pampered years. Her death was by no means predictable. When poor Lazzy finally went off her legs, my father couldn't bear to put her down by the accepted route of breaking her neck, and gave her sufficient sedative to put an elephant to sleep. Lazzy consequently fell into a deep slumber, nursed in my bedroom, and woke up three days later. My father then called in Mike, our vet and good friend, who put Lazzy to rest, finally, in a peaceful, predictable and certain way.

My school years were not exactly a tale of academic success. My brother Andy and I both attended the same school for most of our youth. Neither of us really excelled in any department, though Andy did learn how to smoke a cigarette successfully, and kindly tutored me for a few years until I too had learnt the skill. Fortunately the finances involved in continuing this hobby soon curtailed it, though my brother still flies the flag. Our secondary school, Westcliff High, was close to our home in Leigh-on-Sea. The school was an all boys affair, though fortunately right next door to the girls' school. Andy formed a small punk rock band, and naturally most of my interests followed on from what my big brother was involved in. In my eyes he was the coolest guy on the block.

School was all about learning sport and acquiring a passion for motorcycles, as far as I was concerned. The first motorcycle arrived six weeks before my sixteenth birthday, much to the disappointment of mum and dad. I had saved for months from the money that I had earned from my paper round, and had taken this money in monthly instalments to one of the local motorcycle shops. Here, they had kindly kept a record of the payments until I had given them enough for my dream bike, a seven-year-old Fantic Caballero moped. I was absolutely thrilled at the prospect of no longer relying on pedal-power to get to school and back. Suddenly, I was going to be free. I knew that my parents would not welcome the motorcycle, but fortunately Andy had already taken the heat from the situation by getting one himself. Most of the arguments about how dangerous they are, how noisy and antisocial they are, and how impractical they are, had already taken place. On the day of pick-up, I was not old enough to ride the moped home. I arrived at the shop with my satchel from school, paid my last instalment and then proudly left. I pushed my prize home on the pavement, all five miles, working out how I could conceal it from my parents. I arrived at our house and pushed it through the side gate and into the back garden, and hid it behind one of the sheds. This was to be my moped's home, at least until I had worked out how to break the news to my parents. The plan failed miserably. It was discovered the following day when my father fell over one of its pedals while trying to smoke a cigarette behind the shed in his dressing gown and slippers. For months mother had been harassing him to give up smoking, and he'd informed her that he was well into the process of cleansing his system of the dreaded weed. Clearly, this was not quite true, and as he came in with dirty knees from his tumble, mother remarked that it had been divine justice for telling her fibs. This distracted them both from the fact that their second son was now a motorcycle owner.

At school, I captained the first team in squash, swimming and running, which excited me greatly, but would have excited my parents more if it had been the Debating Society or the Literature Club. I obtained some reasonable qualifications at the school, but my interest in study waned with my teachers' failure to encourage me. For my eighteenth birthday, mum and dad gave me a really generous present, one that they hoped would distract me from the evils of motorised two-wheeled devil machines. They helped me buy a car. We found a lovely gold Ford Escort for £800. I sold my small 100cc motorcycle and put in all of my wages from another morning paper round and some Saturday work cleaning up in a local butcher's shop, and on November 17th 1982 the Escort become my first car. My parents were delighted to see me leaving the perils of two wheels behind, and could now rest easily in their bed secure in the knowledge that neither of their sons were riding motorcycles any more.

Sadly for them this peace of mind was short-lived. I have sometimes been known to be a little impulsive, and mid-March 1983 was one such occasion. After leaving school early one day, I decided to drop into Bikewise, the local motorcycle shop, to say hello to some old friends. There in the window was a stunning Honda 900cc sports bike that looked just fantastic. Foolishly, I asked the shop owner if I could have a ride, and I was hooked. Straddling the large tank, I turned the key and started it up. The deep 'rrroar' from the four-cylinder engine turned my thighs to jelly. I pulled in the clutch, engaged first gear, and let the clutch out with a small twist of the throttle, just like I used to do on my 100cc Suzuki. This resulted in the bike careering up the tarmac with me on board but definitely not in control. As the speed forced me backwards into the seat, my right hand turned the throttle in the 'accelerating' direction, causing another rapid increase in speed. As the traffic lights came into view, the red light clearly signalling that I should stop, I just about managed to regain some sort of control over the beast. When I returned to the shop, I was greeted with smiles and laughter, as owner and staff had witnessed the start of this test ride. I just about calmed down enough to dismount without caving in from the adrenaline. It was hopeless; I just HAD to have it. We agreed on a straight swap for the Ford Escort, and the deal was done. I rode the new Honda home. My parents naturally hit the roof and I suffered several weeks of torment from them over my foolishness. I, however, could not have been happier. I was having a ball on the powerful machine, and knew then that my love affair with two wheels would stay with me for the foreseeable future.

The arrival of my 'A' level results was not a good day at home. Once again, Andy had paved the way and prepared my parents for disappointment on the academic front. He had not fulfilled his potential and neither did I. Studying for the exams had proved a challenge. The lures of a night out on the bikes, or a cosy night in down at the Plough, our local pub, were both far stronger than a night in with the books. The day that my results arrived, I opened them with a half-hearted hope that I would have bluffed my way to some reasonable grades, but no. I attended the local re-sit college. It was a one-year course, and not particularly interesting, however, I stuck at it, and finally sat down in the examination room to try to undo the previous year's misery. The exams went reasonably well, and I came out with sufficient grades to attend London University, Queen Mary's College, where I sat for a degree in Genetics. It was a relatively new subject in 1984, and seemed to be the sort of course which attracted folk who hadn't got high enough qualifications to do a proper degree, which suited me fine.

Financing a life at university was always going to be tricky. In the 1980's the government paid tuition fees for students from the United Kingdom. However, all other funding from the local authority was means-tested so I would not receive any help, as dad's career as a doctor and mum's as a teacher were, understandably, deemed sufficient to provide for their offspring. My parents were great and did what they could, but there would always be a shortfall. At least once a month I had the excitement and relief of receiving a letter from dad, postmarked from his surgery, containing the means to a good weekend, or maybe even a new book or two. He would describe it as his 'ash cash', the fee paid to a General Practitioner for filling in a cremation certificate for a recently deceased patient. While this may appear in somewhat bad taste, it did provide a most welcome addition to my perpetually empty piggy bank.

It was during these years at university that I struck up a long-lasting and healthy relationship with my bank manager. I had approached him during my first year with an idea to turn a modest profit buying and selling motorcycles. I had read and learnt a lot about them by this time. I managed to convince the bank manager to set up a loan account, from which I could draw up to £3,000. This, almost 30 years ago, was a considerable amount of money, so my initial pitch to him must have been a passionate one. I would draw down funds to purchase any motorcycle that I believed was particularly good value, in the hope of selling it on for a moderate profit. For this to have any success, I needed to secure a copy of the weekly Motorcycle News before it became available to the general public. As luck would have it, this newspaper was printed not far from my student digs in the east end of London. On Tuesday afternoon, the string-tied bundles would be prepared for distribution to the newsagents, for sale the following day. However, one stall in the nearby market got their copies on Tuesday evening. By gaining the friendship of the owner of this stall, I was able to procure my copy a day early. I would rush back to the flat, roll myself a cigarette, and ponder and thumb my way through the adverts over and over again, until I had narrowed down the likely bargains of the week. I would then make some phone calls and get myself set for travelling the following day, often long distances, so that I would be the first at the seller's house to view the 'bargain'. It worked well, and I managed to finish my studies at Queen Mary's College with no debt, a happy bank manager, and a certain amount of pride that I had not continually turned up at my parents' door with an empty hand and a deep pocket.

I kept up with the squash, running and hiking, and finally found the trick to doing well in exams. It appeared that the harder I worked, the better the marks that I achieved. I don't know why I didn't hit on this earlier, but I started to take pride in getting good results. I graduated in 1987 with a First Class Honours degree. It was great to see my parents proud and I started doing a PhD in Genetics, but soon became bored with it. After much deliberation, I narrowed my future down to Medicine. Of course, I shall never know whether I chose the correct path at that time, but I have always firmly believed that one should never look back with regret, only forward with enthusiasm, and this has been the case with my career in medicine.

I had an interview at Aberdeen Medical School and loved it there, so my heart was set. I had a fabulous five years training there, and delighted my parents by graduating at the top of the class. It almost seemed paradoxical to me, that the teachers at Westcliff High School for Boys used to tell me that I would never make anything of myself, yet here I was achieving the highest marks in medical exams. It wasn't a 'well, I'll show them' syndrome, more of a 'well, I was just messing around then, and learning what life was about' syndrome. I understand that spending much of one's youth in local pubs playing for the darts teams, or riding around on motorbikes is not necessarily the secret of future academic success, but for me it was all part of growing up. I really have no regrets about the path that my life took.

It was while I was at Aberdeen that my interest in mountaineering was re-kindled. I joined the Mountaineering Society at the University, and thoroughly enjoyed our frequent forays into the Grampian Mountains and Highlands of Scotland. I was developing a love of open spaces and brief encounters with dangerous places. The more exposed and unforgiving the territory, the greater the sense of well-being I experienced from successfully negotiating adverse situations.

I met Clare, my wife, whilst working at Aberdeen Royal Infirmary after graduation. I was teaching the morning that we met, and she was a young, feisty Glaswegian in her third year of medicine. As she palpated a patient's abdomen, she remarked, 'Dr Sutcliffe, are you looking at my cleavage?' I was guilty, and that was it, I was hooked.

My first meeting with Peggy, Clare's mother, was an interesting one. Clare had been previously settled in a long relationship with a chap called Rob, who had well and truly gained Peggy's favour. Peggy and David, her husband, were good friends with Rob's parents, so I was already batting from a sticky wicket. I hit it off well with David. He had been an accomplished road runner, and by this time, I was participating in regular half and full marathons, so our conversation eased effortlessly into this field. Peggy on the other hand, tactfully announced, 'Well, you've got cheeky eyes and a good sense of humour, I can see what Clare sees in you... I think. But you're not Rob!' It took a little while for us to see eye to eye, but hopefully, it no longer concerns her that I am not Rob!

Then it was Clare's turn for initiation into the Sutcliffe household. Shortly after we started seeing each other, we travelled back to Leigh-on-Sea for Clare to meet my parents, Andy and Lara, my sister. The drive down from Aberdeen had taken fourteen hours, and we arrived close to midnight. I let us both into the darkened hallway, I fumbled my way to the light switch and flicked it on. A shriek from Clare informed me that she had met my father, presenting himself to her for the first time sporting nothing more than some rather tight grey cotton briefs, the waist band being tucked away neatly under the crease of the lowered and somewhat protruding anterior abdominal wall that creeps up on many of us as we get older. Oh, and a pair of off-white ankle socks. He held out both arms and welcomed Clare into the house, as only dad could, with nothing but love and affection in his warm smile. Clare nervously accepted the offer, embracing my father fully from the mid-torso upwards, but flexing slightly at her hips so as not to intrude too much onto the front of his briefs. Mum came downstairs, immediately ordered father to put his clothes on, and gave us both a welcoming hug. We had a great weekend at home, and Clare got on really well with my family. Andy made her laugh for the duration, and Lara talked non-stop, as is her way.

Once I'd finished my undergraduate days, I felt a burden had been lifted. I was now free. Free from the continuous revision, free from the constant presentations, and free from the constraints of general poverty and medical school life. I started on some postgraduate training in Oxford, but found the distance between Clare and me very difficult. Leaving Oxford on a Friday at 5pm, I wouldn't get to Aberdeen before 1am Saturday morning. Exhausted from the drive, I'd flop into bed, wake up late in the afternoon, and go out with Clare in the evening, then return to Oxford on Sunday morning. We did it for almost a year, but that was long enough. Much to the annoyance of the medical staff, I was the first person to drop off the medical rotation at that eminent hospital. I returned to Aberdeen, and could not have been happier. On the drive back up the motorway, away from the towers and spires of one of the world's finest centres for medicine, I wore the broadest of smiles.

From the day that I arrived at the world-renowned John Radcliffe Hospital, I had never really settled in. As I entered the 'on-call' ward, I was handed a scruffy sheet of paper by an utterly exhausted young man in a white coat. This young doctor had just finished his weekend on-call, and had worked from 6pm on Friday evening until 8am Monday morning without a break. He had not slept, had hardly eaten, looked dehydrated and somewhat confused with fatigue. 'Thank God you're here', he exclaimed, 'Here's the list of new patients that I've not seen yet.' And with that, he left the room, presumably to collapse into the nearest bed. I looked at the sheet of paper and counted fifty-six names: these were the new patients that had not been seen. The doctor going off call had seen well over a hundred and thirty new admissions over the weekend, and this was what remained.

That was how it was at the hospital when on-call: there was never any peace, never any slack, never a break. I was certainly not afraid of hard work, but this was, quite frankly, unsafe and inhuman. It was impossible to talk to the consultants about it, as the 'Well, it'll do you no harm and I did it at your stage' reply would be all too obvious. The fact was that, actually, not one of them had ever worked to that level of intensity in their earlier careers. Medicine has moved on greatly in recent years, and the multitude of new tests that were required by that point had dramatically increased the workload. The whole process was frustrating, exhausting and utterly demoralising. As well as looking after several wards, undertaking an all-too-frequent on-call rota, and trying to get some sleep, I also had to prepare for regular presentations to the entire medical staff at the hospital.

These presentations went on monthly and were very uncomfortable. The chosen doctor would prepare some cases, transfer them to slides, present them to the staff of consultants and juniors, and then get torn to pieces by aloof, pompous physicians trying to score points against their colleagues and show everyone how intelligent they were by asking some question that the presenter couldn't answer. That in itself would not have been too traumatic for me, but at my first presentation to over a hundred people, one of my 'colleagues' thought it would be most amusing to steal my slides from the projector minutes before I was due to start. Consequently, I welcomed the masses into the auditorium and 'clicked up' my opening slide – and nothing happened. What followed next was just awful. I had no presentation to deliver and all of my hard work between on-call, ward cover and sleep had been wasted. It had been difficult enough trying to integrate into Oxford, as the hospital rarely took 'outsiders' from Aberdeen. Now, the doubters had their justification. I made the best of a very bad job, and talked my way through thirty minutes of the expected hour, but it was not a good presentation for obvious reasons. After that, I'd had enough of this particular centre of 'academic excellence'. For the following seven months, I planned my exit. The whole experience had been thoroughly unpleasant; if it hadn't been for my flat-mate Mike and his humour, I would have walked out long before I did. Leaving was the right decision. I'd never been more sure of a decision in my life.

Clare and I moved in together, and our relationship went from strength to strength. Our first date had been to a tiny pub in Pennan, a small coastal fishing village made famous by the film Local Hero. We'd really enjoyed ourselves that evening, and it felt appropriate to return to the delightful village to propose to Clare. My mother had kindly offered me my grandmother's engagement ring, of amethyst and pearl, mounted in gold. This was lovely, as I had no money and plenty of debt, having not long graduated. On the drive to Pennan, I wondered whether Clare suspected anything, as I was definitely fidgety. We arrived and parked up, overlooking a rough sea; waves breaking against the stone walls of the harbour, spraying the air with a white, salty mist. I wasted no time; I couldn't wait any longer. We walked over towards the harbour and along the harbour wall. I stopped halfway along, and turned to face Clare. 'I have something to ask you,' I announced. She looked a little surprised. 'What's that, Ali?' she asked. I knelt down on one knee. 'Will you marry me?' I asked. Clare looked at me and her face lit up in the moonlight. She was wearing a huge smile, and crouched down to meet me, kissed me and replied, 'Of course I will.' We walked, hand in hand, back to the pub, and enjoyed... not a glass of anything bubbly but a hot cup of coffee, just as we had done one year before.

The wedding date coincided with Clare's graduation from medical school. She too had come top in her studies. I was deeply proud of her achievement and knew that great things lay ahead for her. She was intelligent, attractive and liked by everyone, and, amazingly, she had said 'yes' to my proposal of marriage. Our wedding day was a riotous affair. As well as the family and close friends, over two hundred medical graduates turned up uninvited. The hotel staff, far from being disturbed and irritated by the mass of gatecrashers, very kindly put on a huge buffet for the 'extra guests', free of charge. When I apologised to the hotel manager, he actually shook my hand and thanked me for the most profitable night that the hotel had experienced in its fourteen-year history. Apparently, all three bars had been drunk dry by the revellers – what a relief! By the time we got to the bridal suite at the hotel, I was ready to consummate our marriage. As we sat down on the bed, Clare asked if I could help her out of her wedding dress, which involved starting at the most northerly button of the basque and working my way southwards. It was during this tender moment, with just a hint of a whispered warning, 'Oh God! I'm completely knackered!' that she managed to fall into a deep sleep. Fortunately, the hotel was equipped with satellite television, and I immersed myself in a live basketball match. Whoever said that romance was dead was clearly mistaken. Consoled by my brother-in-law Toni's assertion that 'real men consummate on the second night', I slipped off to sleep carefully nursing the remote control.

Clare comes from a large family, having four brothers, and two sisters. They are close, and look after each other, generally appearing en masse at festive occasions. They are good people, and it was great to see our families together at the wedding. The broad Scottish accents of Clare's family were ever tolerant of the Southerners on my side, asking if they could just repeat that sentence or word once more, having not quite understood it at the four previous attempts. I was heartened by a reminder from one of the brothers to 'never hurt ma baby sis else you'll hafti explain yersel tae all o' us!'

Shortly after the wedding, a job came up for a General Practitioner in Whitby, a small northern seaside town. I'd never heard of it, but we decided to travel down for an interview. It looked like a good opportunity, so Clare and I thought we'd take a look. The interview went well, I loved the place and the job, and the practice seemed to like me. I accepted the offer of a job.

The move would fit in with Clare's plans too. She had long harboured the dream of becoming a surgeon, a dream that would require an obsessive dedication to be realised successfully. No other career in medicine demands such complete determination, especially as it's such a male-dominated profession. While we had both graduated with Firsts, mine had been through a lot of hard work and a good slice of luck; Clare, on the other hand, was undoubtedly gifted with academic excellence. She was unusual, a very special person indeed. She had the ability to touch everyone that she came into contact with, in a way that made me feel most proud, and still bemused as to why she had agreed to be my lifelong partner. To this day, I can think of no other person who would be prepared to put up with the sort of nonsense that Clare has had to endure.

The move to Whitby was fantastic for many reasons, but the development of my figure was not one of them. My friend and partner at the practice, John, has a wife who bakes exceptionally good cakes. I found out about this shortly after moving to North Yorkshire, and started purchasing a fine selection of chocolate sponges, flapjacks and pastries from her regularly on a Friday morning. The plan was simple. I would allow myself one, or at the most two, of these delicacies after morning surgery on the Friday, and skip lunch that day. I would then take the majority back home, where I would share them with Clare and our next-door neighbours. However, the plan had a major flaw: my self-control. I found myself unable to resist the bounty that sat under my desk and often left for home empty-handed after evening surgery. This resulted in Clare and the others missing out on the baked delights, and had a disastrous effect on my previously flat stomach. Within three months I had gained nearly three stones in weight, and found myself increasingly breathless on the squash court and on the receiving end of several comments from the more 'forward' members of my patient list.

It was at a millennium party in Glasgow that Peggy's husband David did me an immeasurable favour. The day after the party, we were reviewing some of David's videos from the previous evening, when we came across a moving image of a figure that I didn't recognise from the party. The man, standing six foot tall, had his shirt tail untucked, looked a little the worse for wear from alcohol and was smoking a cigar. He had a large, unattractive overhang of fat protruding from the top of an over-tightened belt, and the creases where the back of his chest wall met the lumbar region were clearly visible through the ruffled-up sides of his dress shirt. His thighs were large enough to stop any light from passing until the knees, and the trousers were curled around the back of his shoes, having been forced down by the pressure from the abdomen. When this mysterious guest turned round to face the video camera, I was horrified to recognise the face as my own. This was the wake-up call that I had needed; I immediately started planning my rehabilitation.

The next twenty-four months were hard work. Not at the practice, but getting myself back into shape. Early morning runs became the norm, which delighted the dogs, and Clare and I set by running several half and full marathons. I had truly been embarrassed about the images that I'd seen that morning in January when we had reviewed the videos from the party, and I vowed to never let myself drift back into that position. I found that the running was inspirational for many reasons. It was 'our' time, when Clare and I could be free from the pressures of work and could talk to each other without constant interruptions from phones or pagers. It was something that we truly enjoyed doing together. On the occasions when I ran on my own, just with the dogs, it provided me with time to reflect on life, and to look to the future and dream about what it might hold. It gave me time to work through all sorts of issues, whether it was the conundrums of patient health or my own rehabilitation to a healthy lifestyle. The weight soon dropped away, and a year later I was able to once again complete a half marathon in under 1hr 45mins. Life was getting back on track, but I certainly missed those fabulous cakes.

It was during 2001-2002 that I first developed a relationship with St Catherine's Hospice. Based in Scarborough, it treats many patients with various terminal diseases, and provides a great deal of support to the families and friends of its patients at the time when they need it the most. As I started to compete in more full and half marathons, I tried at every opportunity to raise awareness of the Hospice, whenever possible raising funds in the process through the generous contributions of friends, family and the local community in Whitby. This relationship was to continue for many years.

In December 2002, sitting back in our house in North Yorkshire, already dark outside as it approached 4pm, I looked at my bookcase packed full of interesting mountaineering books, factual discussions of survival, success and failure from all over the globe. 'What happened to your climbing ambitions?' I asked myself. Climbing had, in previous years, opened up a new universe to me. It involved all of my senses: the touch and feel of the various rock faces; the sounds of the mountains, whether listening for an approaching avalanche or the crunch of crystallized ice and snow underfoot; the smells from the summits as tiny spicules of ice crystals invaded my nasal cavities, blown there by a tormenting wind; the taste of the air, laced with fragrances from the valley flora; and finally the sights – sights of almost indescribable beauty, of a perfect windless warm summit day contrasting with the savagery of an unrelenting storm front tearing its way through an unprepared camp. The camaraderie that exists between climbers is unimaginable, the 'brotherhood of the rope' binding all who travel together on it with the same set of unwritten rules. Occasionally, there is the opportunity to lay a path where no-one else has previously trodden. Along with all of these things there is an obsession with what the view will look like from the summit. These were the reasons that I climbed.

'Well, you went to medical school, where you found all the excuses you needed not to find the time to plan any expeditions, becoming lazy in the process' was my answer. I got to thinking about where I would go, and that was it, I was poring through my old books once again with an eagerness I hadn't experienced since my first ride on a motorcycle. My mouth dry with anticipation, my fingers leaving a slight residue on the crinkled and stained pages, my heart quickening as each destination appeared before me. I was like a child staring at an open box of chocolates at Christmas. I studied these books well, and discussed my intentions with Clare. I was going to start some serious climbing, and could not wait to set about the challenge. As a re-introduction to the skills that I'd now forgotten, I decided to look at getting onto an expedition to The Alps, to climb Mont Blanc.

Mont Blanc stands at 15,782 feet high, and lies on the border of France and Italy. It is the highest mountain in the Alps and Western Europe. The height varies from year to year, depending on the depth of snow at the summit's cap. Its rock summit, under snow and ice, is 15,720 feet, and lies 140 feet below the snow-capped summit. The summit is reached by twenty thousand climbers a year, and consequently lays claim to being one of the world's most deadly mountains. Each year fifty or more lives are lost on its slopes. This was to be my first adventure to serious altitude. Mont Blanc is largely recognised as a sensible springboard into the world of high altitude mountaineering, a climb that can be negotiated with little technical knowledge but one that will test the physical and mental endurance of all those who wish to reach its summit.

The preparation began weeks before, and so did the first creeping of self-doubt. In retrospect, I am glad that these doubts presented themselves early in my high-altitude climbing career, for there would be no place for them later. I had recurring concerns about my adaptability to the rigours. Ben Nevis, 4,409 feet, had been the highest that I'd previously climbed, so this would be a massive increase in altitude. I'd read that the ability to climb to altitude is not necessarily directly related to a person's fitness. Indeed, it is often the case that the fittest person on the team at sea level may be the one that struggles the most up high in the mountains. I was tormented by the thought of failure, of not succeeding at the first big climb in the plan that I was formulating for myself. I would feel completely disillusioned and embarrassed if this first real adventure failed. I wanted it to be a success; I really wanted it to be a success. It became an obsession. I realised early on in my climbing career that to fail because of poor equipment or a lack of proper preparation is a complete waste of everyone's time, effort and money. I was not going to let one of these reasons be an excuse for my failure, and so my training was rigorous. Mornings were spent varying my now well-established dawn runs with the dogs and Clare with hill runs, extended walks with a fully-laden rucksack on my back, and gym sessions. The schedule that I set for myself was punishing, but I drew confidence from seeing my performance getting stronger. If the climb didn't have a successful outcome, then I wanted to be sure it was not because I was ill-prepared.

Without realising it, Clare was becoming excluded from this part of my life. Eventually, the extended time that I put into preparing myself fully for the trip imposed on our quality time together. I spoke with Clare and asked her how she felt about the forthcoming expedition. She knew how focussed I became with challenges such as these – I had, after all, run many marathons and climbed many smaller mountains by this stage. My focus was absolute, but I felt it had to be that way. It was hugely important to me to leave for the expedition with her blessing and not to have any unfinished business between us. There was always the chance that an accident could happen, that I could fall or suffer some disaster on the slopes, and I wanted us to have no regrets about my decision to go. It was what I wanted, but I also wanted her acceptance of this need I had to fulfil my dreams. The candid discussions continued and my wish was granted. I was going with all of Clare's blessings, but I was in no doubt that each winter from now on we would be going on a skiing holiday, for this was her love, and woe betide me should I find any excuse not to accompany her. This seemed absolutely fair, and to date I have kept my side of this agreement.

I'd searched through various websites, finding out as much as I could about the mountain, and tried to gather sufficient climbing kit to see me safely through the expedition. I'd decided to use what gear I had already accumulated during my university years, most of which was excellent, thus avoiding the unnecessary expense of a whole new wardrobe for the expedition. I had confidence in this equipment, but promised myself a refit of the climbing wardrobe if all went according to plan on Mont Blanc.

The expedition started in June 2003, and was set to last eighteen days. The team met up in Chamonix, at a small hotel that offered fine views of our objective from most of the windows. There were six of us on the team including Rob, our guide. With just one female amongst us, it was apparent from our initial friendly exchanges that that the high levels of testosterone being exuded by the other climbers could prove both interesting and entertaining, if not a little challenging. By its nature, mountaineering often attracts slightly egocentric personalities. All those who participate in the sport deny this, but from countless expeditions I can confirm that this is a reasonable reflection. Our Mont Blanc team came from all walks of life, and we were very mixed in our previous climbing experience. As the mountain is largely considered to be a relatively straightforward climb, we all expected to get to the summit and back. Rob echoed these expectations as he went through our itinerary carefully with us. I liked Rob. He was clearly an experienced climber and we enjoyed a similar 'alternative' sense of humour. He stood about 5 feet 10 inches tall, wiry and lithe, his hair unkempt and face unshaven, complementing his chosen career as an outdoor mountain clinician. His arms were tanned and thickset, fingernails cracked and chipped from rock battles and his jeans torn off at the knee – not in some rudimentary attempt to appear trendy, but to clear the cumbersome denim from his knees. He had a firm handshake and I like that. I think it reflects purpose, decisiveness and leadership, all good qualities for someone in his chosen profession. We planned to climb Mont Velan as an acclimatisation hike, take a rest day, then climb Mont Blanc, weather permitting. Mont Velan is situated between the Aosta Valley and the Vallese. Located between Italy and Switzerland, it can be climbed from different sides. We planned to climb it from the Italian side, and in doing so make use of huts on the route for overnight stays. Its summit stands 12,152 feet high and dominates the immediate skyline.

The climb itself was very hard work. The pace that Rob set for us on the ascent was right at the upper level of my comfort zone, and by the time we reached the overnight hut before attempting the summit I, along with most of the team, was exhausted. I felt that I was unprepared for the physical nature of the trip, and vowed that if my body coped well with the altitude then I would get myself considerably fitter for future climbs. The following day's ascent went without a problem and the views from the summit were spectacular. We had been graced with fine weather throughout the two days' climbing, and returned to Chamonix full of hope for our ascent of Mont Blanc.

We duly took our rest day and recovered from the relatively rapid ascent of Mont Velan. Rob detailed the importance of rehydration and eating properly on the mountain, and set about gathering some last minute provisions for the trip. Rob and I got on well, and talked together for many hours. He'd held a job as an engineer before becoming a climbing guide, and clearly the career change suited him. He'd successfully climbed to the summit of Broad Peak, a mountain located on the Pakistani/Chinese border which, at 26,414 feet, stands as the world's twelfth highest mountain. This impressed me a great deal; I had no idea how anyone could climb to that height, having just been totally exhausted by reaching the lowly heights of Mont Velan.

We set off the following day for Mont Blanc. I'd skied in the Alps before, but this was different. The utter vastness engulfed me. The huge irregular backbone running through the skeleton of Western Europe made the trips I'd previously experienced in the area seem like small slopes. Mont Blanc itself dominated all views around Chamonix. It was a giant, immense and standing proud, staring down on all of its sibling slopes shadowing and protecting them from the searing heat of the summer sun and the ravages of the intense, unforgiving winter storms. The initial stages of the climb were fairly straightforward, involving hiking, walking over scree, and a little scrambling, necessitating the use of hand and footholds on the rock. Most was on frozen wasteland, interspersed with crumbling rocks and shale. We reached the overnight hut on the Dome de Gouter route in the early evening. We had chosen this route because our original plan to traverse the North East Ridge via Mont Maudit and Mont Blanc du Tacul had been blighted by adverse weather conditions. Once in the hut, one of the team members, Alex, announced that he had been struggling with the altitude. He had previously climbed Kilimanjaro, Africa's highest mountain at 19,340 feet, so this came as a surprise to both Alex and the rest of the team. Rob did what he could to assess him, and decided that descent was the most sensible option. He advised Alex not to attempt the summit with the rest of us the following day, and we would all descend as a team on our return. I did wonder at the time whether the speed of our ascent on both Mont Velan and Mont Blanc had anything to do with Alex's condition. We spent a miserable night in the vastly overcrowded hut. There was no room for us to lay down our sleeping bags and sleep was just impossible, because of the noise and the kerosene fumes that filled the hut and gave everyone a headache.

We set off at 3am, just before dawn, to make the most of the firm and relatively stable snow and ice bridges along our path. With head torches on and hearts thumping, we left the hut and set our cramponed boots on the virgin snow outside. It was a beautiful night, the stars sparkling brightly above, and the moon casting its glow on the icy wilderness in front of my beam of light. The silence was broken from time to time by one of us coughing as the freezing air hit our lungs. The pace was different on that day, much slower than Rob had previously set. A steady, upward climb toward the summit, taking breaks every couple of hours to drink and eat. Daybreak, welcomed by all, cast warmth on our chilled bodies and refreshed our enthusiasm for the task ahead. Slowly and steadily we progressed up the hill, until at 11am we could climb no higher. As the team stood on top of Mont Blanc, my happiness was dominated by a feeling of relief. Relief that my body seemed to be able to cope with the altitude and effort required to get there, relief that the trip had, so far, been successful, and relief that we would soon be heading down. I stopped for a short while on the summit, plunging my ice axe firmly into the snow, and took time to look around. The view was magnificent, with fantastic snow-capped peaks piercing the air at irregular intervals along the backbone of The Alps. It was the best view I had ever seen, anywhere, and I was in it, in the moment of that view. It felt perfect. I was utterly triumphant.

The descent went without a hitch. We gathered Alex from the hut on the way down and retreated back to the village. That evening we revelled in the views, drank some fine wine, and I amused myself watching the wine and beer take control as some of the guys on the team vied for the attentions of our single female team member. We talked about our future plans. I was hooked and really, really wanted to organise another expedition.

CLARE

I was only nineteen when I met Ali and had no intention of settling down and entering anything serious, but by the third date I knew I would end up marrying him. Ali was completely different from my previous boyfriends, a little eccentric, but he made me laugh, which is the key to a successful long-term relationship. When we first met, I was in my third year of university and was supporting myself by working in pubs and nightclubs. Ali had just qualified and was working over one hundred hours a week, so our 'dates' usually consisted of nights watching a video huddled up on the sofa and wondering who would fall asleep first! When we had some time off, we used to head into the Highlands in Ali's 1974 pale blue Ford Cortina and spend the days walking. I loved that car and Ali gave it to me on the day I qualified from medical school. Although we had no money and our joint possessions could fit into two black bin liners, they were undoubtedly some of the happiest times of our life.

The first few years of our married life flew by as we were both doing long hours at the hospital. It is no surprise that the divorce rates of two married doctors exceed fifty percent as the early part of your career demands so much time and effort. When you are not working, you are studying for post-graduate exams. One day, Ali came home with a one-carat diamond ring. When we had got engaged two years before, he gave me his Grandmother's amethyst and pearl ring, as there was no money to buy a new one. I did like this ring, but as he had given it to two other girls before me, I made him promise to buy me one of my own in the future! After presenting me with this gift, he announced that he wanted to apply for a job in Yorkshire. I was very concerned. A few weeks earlier, I had obtained a position on Aberdeen's surgical training programme and did not want to give it up. A few of my consultant bosses told me that if I left, my surgical career would be finished. Ali was so set on the idea of a move, however, that I decided to keep these feelings to myself and followed him down south. I managed to get a job in a local hospital and things worked out, although I spent several years commuting long distances to get the training I required.

It is difficult to tell your partner, in a sensitive way, that they are putting on weight. I would often joke with Ali that he was becoming cuddly and pointed out that I was buying him size 40 inch waist trousers instead of 34!

When he saw the home video footage, he instantly changed his lifestyle. He stopped smoking, started running and playing squash regularly. Ali has some obsessive personality traits and when he sets his mind to a task, nothing will stop him achieving his goal. He thrived on the natural, endorphin-induced highs that exercise gave him and, even to this day, if he misses a run, he becomes pretty hard to live with! When he told me he was off to Mont Blanc, I thought this was a one-off physical challenge and had no idea that high-altitude mountaineering was about to take over our lives.

Chapter 2
Aconcagua

Clare and I had had several long and testing discussions on my return home from Mont Blanc. She had never doubted that the trip would be a success, but I don't think she had bought into the concept of 'the mountaineer husband' as yet. Within two days of my return, I was talking with her about Aconcagua, but my thoughts did not stop there. Deep down, I yearned to climb Mount Everest one day. I didn't discuss it ever, with anyone, for fear of being ridiculed. But I just knew that one day I'd get the chance. Clare could see how totally focussed I was becoming. I understood her concerns – the safety, the long periods away from home, the emptiness she would feel in the house – but somehow they didn't fully register with me. Mountaineering is an expensive hobby and I was lucky I had the ability to work extra shifts on call to fund my expeditions. The night shifts were exhausting but I was desperate to return to the landscape of mountains and valleys. I'd found something that I loved, had always longed to do, and could do successfully.

I felt sure that Clare would understand that the long nights away working and training were worth it, but I forgot to ever really ask her. After all, it was Clare who would be left running the house in my absence and she would be left without her best friend on her holidays, as my own holidays would be eaten away with climbing expeditions. I should have talked to her more about this at the time and I regret not doing so. I tried on many occasions to discuss with her what climbing really meant to me, but often failed. I wanted to explain to her the significance of climbing in my life, but at the same time reassure her that she was, and would always be, the most important thing in my life. Somehow, I knew she understood some aspects of what I said, but didn't want to understand the reasons behind them. After all, why could I possibly want to work all of these extra shifts, doing long hours away from home, to finance a hobby that carried a well-recognised risk of not returning home, and enforced separation between two people who loved each other? I could understand why it would make no sense, but then nor do many other pursuits, such as training all your life to be the fastest around a running track, or to jump the furthest in a sand pit, unless it is you that is striving for it. The complete dedication required to be successful in such pursuits is totally absorbing. Success in some aspects of life often occurs at the expense of a wider perspective and broader appreciation of the complexities of life. But that success comes an inner calm that is difficult to describe although it is understood by those fortunate enough to experience it, no matter what the circumstances.

I'd been a partner at Whitby Group Practice for four years by this time, and Clare was smoothly rising through the ranks from junior surgeon to Registrar. Her rotation consisted of numerous cross-county drives to Hull, Leeds, Northallerton and Scarborough in all seasons, through rain, sun and snow. She would often leave the house at 5am and return long after dark, working every other weekend. I continued training hard to prepare myself for the mountains once more. This chaotic lifestyle that we now led somehow worked, as we each knew we had the complete support of the other.

Aconcagua, I decided, was the ideal first real high-altitude destination. Standing at 22,835 feet, this giant is the highest mountain in the Western Hemisphere. On the Argentinean-Chilean border, it is a massive crumbling volcanic peak, consisting of varied routes, glaciers, seracs, ridges and odd-shaped *penitentes*, tall ice spikes left from glacial melt. The Vacas Valley, a lesser-used twenty-mile hike, would be the preferred entrance to base camp and the surrounding amphitheatre that Aconcagua presents to all those who attempt to stand on its giant shoulders.

And so, in December of 2002, I set off for the start of the expedition. The night before departure had been a difficult one. Clare and I had argued about something trivial, but it had upset my karma. I needed us to be on good terms with each other for the following day's goodbye session, but now found myself alone in our bed, deserted by Clare and the dogs. Clare was in the spare room. This was all wrong, and preyed heavily on my mind. After an hour or two, I left my bed to speak with her. I was always conscious, the night before I set off on an expedition, that if some disaster were to happen it could be our last night together. I hoped Clare never thought this way, but we never spoke about the possible consequences of my pursuit of self-fulfilment. We talked until the early hours, both expressing ourselves and working out how we had arrived at separate bedrooms that night. I think Clare was starting to feel that my love for climbing was encroaching on our relationship. I sensed this, and mentally noted that I would need be more sensitive to her needs, and not just follow my own, if these adventures were to continue with her blessing. We cuddled, made up and settled down in our bed together again. The dogs, realising that the voices had now returned to their normal placid levels, crept back up the stairs and gently pawed themselves back on top of the duvet, so that the pack could once more be complete.

I was nervous when I got off the plane in Mendoza. Had the entire luggage that I'd so carefully crammed into the duffel bags arrived with me at the airport? What were my climbing partners going to be like – we'd never met before, but had come together through one of the world's leading climbing outfits, International Mountain Guides (IMG) – and were they all going to be in better shape and have more experience than me? My anxieties were soon put into perspective as I turned around in the airport to a shout of 'Hey, is that Alistair Sutcliffe from the UK?' I stand at six foot but felt dwarfed by the man who'd thrown his voice across the small airport's arrival area. This was Mark Tucker, lead guide for the expedition and one of the most experienced guides at IMG. 'Yep,' I replied hesitantly, as other arrivals in the airport did their best to ignore my obvious embarrassment at hearing my name shouted at such volume. After gathering my kit bags with anticipation and breathing sighs of relief that everything was present and correct, we headed off with some other team members to the small but friendly hotel that we'd be using to check through our gear and discuss the impending expedition.

An eclectic bunch, with interests ranging from business to neuro-surgery; this was our climbing group, and we all tried nervously to get to know each other. After all, we'd be eating, drinking, climbing, sleeping and occasionally toileting together over the next three weeks. The group dynamics are always interesting. 'You can never get on with all of the people all of the time', my father used to say. And how true this is. I instantly clicked with the neurosurgeon, probably because we had medicine in common, and I was fascinated by his open discussion with me of the medication that he would feel comfortable taking during the climb if necessary. Dexamethasone, a steroid only used in emergencies on the mountain, for patients with cerebral oedema, swelling of the brain due to altitude, would be on his diet. I dared not question him on this, as he was an experienced neurosurgeon and had vast experience of using the drug with his patients post-surgery, but I couldn't help but wonder: if he got into trouble, how would the guides know what to use if he's been nibbling on Dexamethasone as we proceed up the hill? The others in the group all had their stories to tell, and we all listened patiently to each other, contemplating privately whether he or she made us feel at ease or on edge.

People often believe that the climber's worst enemies high up on the mountain are avalanches and falls into crevasses. However, it is the body's metabolic responses to high altitude conditions that are the greatest threat to the mountaineer. The most feared of these are pulmonary oedema and cerebral oedema. In cerebral oedema, the brain swells and the cerebellum, the part of the brain responsible for balance and co-ordination becomes constricted in the base of the skull, the body is no longer able to perform these functions effectively, resulting in the climber staggering, becoming disorientated, and often falling. On many occasions, this can lead to a fatal slip, or unconsciousness through squeezing of the brain. Pulmonary oedema, if it can't be reversed results in the climber drowning in their own secretions and fluids. Medical and physiological treatments can help these conditions, but the only real treatment is always descent, as quickly as possible, followed by urgent expert medical treatment.

Mark sat us all down the next morning and ran through the detailed itinerary with his team. We discussed the basics of the climb, the kit-check, and the hike itself. We would set off the following morning to start the long hike to base camp. I wondered whether I was really ready for this. Some of the team had already been to this mountain before, and my résumé read pitifully compared to the others. The highest I'd ever been was Mont Blanc. I had had no problems at that altitude, but how would I cope climbing to over six thousand feet higher? Nerves aside, there was only one way to find out, and I was there now, so decided to see how high I could get.

The hotel that we had used for our base was a drab affair. Stuffy rooms with occasionally-hot water, two beds separated by a few inches of floor space, a table and a light, with a window for the lucky few. The linen for the beds had surely been purchased from the local ranch cowboys – hessian in texture, made from horse hair, it infiltrated any available skin crack or chafe that it could find, made all the more unpleasant in night-time temperatures of 90 degrees Fahrenheit. The shared shower, and I use the singular deliberately, spent its life billowing filthy water from its hairy hole, desperately asking anyone who dipped their sand and dirt-ridden bodies into its depths to bend down and release the thick plait of multicoloured keratin and fluff from it, and let it breathe once more. But nobody dared, and rightly so, for God only knew what disease lurked in the matted mass. I was only too happy to leave when the time came.

We set off the following day at 8am, after a healthy breakfast. 'Peel everything' Mark had warned us. Gastroenteritis on an expedition can be a disaster. It spreads swiftly through a healthy group of climbers, rendering fit individuals useless within hours. At the start of the Vacas Valley hike in to base camp, Mark grouped us all together. 'Try to keep together on the trail, keep your eyes open for rock falls and bandits, drink plenty, and enjoy yourselves. This is the last point that you can turn around without causing a nuisance. Your choice!'

Quietly we looked at each other – was anyone going to take up Tuck's offer? We all turned 90 degrees, put our caps on, and started the three-day hike to Aconcagua base camp.

The trek in to base camp was uneventful apart from a brush with two bandits on horseback. They approached our team, demanded money and brandished a small penknife at Mark in a threatening manner. I was terrified. Their scarred faces grimaced at this wandering bunch of tourists, seemingly offering easy pickings. Their black, decaying teeth interspersed with holes and irregular slivers of gold, preventing some, but not all, of the bubbling saliva from falling out of the corners of their stubbled smiles. One bore a large, purple-coloured lesion on the right hand side of his lower lip. 'A basal cell carcinoma', I thought to myself, 'or maybe even a melanoma' – the latter being swiftly fatal if left untreated. But this was not the time or the place to lay down my inflatable bed and offer this patient a consultation. Then, completely unmoved by these two thieves, Mark produced a large hunting knife with a twelve-inch blade from the back of his waistband, and brandished it at our would-be robbers. They shouted, turned their horses around swiftly and rode off, back into the cloud of dust that they'd produced on their arrival. Mark had clearly hiked here before. The Crocodile Dundee moment seemed humorous at the time, but the consequences if Mark had not known the territory could have been more serious.

By the end of day three, we were lying in our two-man tents, busily arranging our gear into neat piles within the constraints of our nylon homes. The climb proper would consist of forays from our base camp in the Guanocos valley (13,000 feet) up to camp 1 (14,500 feet), camp 2 (17,800 feet), camp 3 (19,500 feet), and then attempt the summit at 22,835 feet. Between each settlement at a new camp, there would be various hikes up the mountain and retreats to lower altitudes, thus assisting our acclimatisation and fitness for the task of summit day. We had two contingency days built into our plan, in case of bad weather or sickness. Should all proceed to plan, then by day twenty we'd be safely back at the hotel, enjoying a celebratory meal, with the memory of the summit of Aconcagua lodged firmly into our cerebral cortexes.

Tent etiquette has its own rulebook. Tidiness is paramount, bodily functions should be performed with consideration, no bringing snow into the tent, and snoring is permitted but deeply frowned upon. Unfortunately for my tent partner on this expedition, I was not aware of such formalities and apparently disobeyed all the rules for the first couple of nights. However, the group of eight was soon gelling well, looking out for each other and sharing life stories after the day's climbing was done. Day eight brought our first retirements, two friends from the USA who had travelled over to climb the mountain together. Both had succumbed to back pain, a recurrence of previous problems unrelieved by the medication that both they and I carried, and also unresponsive to some impromptu deep massage therapy given by a willing female participant from another climbing team. This injury didn't surprise me, as our tents were pitched on a rock plateau and our rucksacks were heavily laden with climbing gear. While every effort was made to flatten the 'floor' of the tent as much as possible, inevitably loose rocks find their way into the softest part of your back just as REM sleep starts, initiating a roulette wheel of a sleep/waking cycle that is difficult to break. By morning, the combination of cold, sleep deprivation, muscle aches and altitude cough create an interesting and sometimes unenthusiastic start to the day.

We had all soon grown accustomed to the toileting procedure. Part of the fee for the climbing permit is paid to the Aconcagua National

Park. For this modest fee we were allowed the privilege of some privacy during bowel evacuation. They provided blue cubicles with a toilet 'hole', consisting of two strips of wood on which one would balance, crouch, and then let nature take its course. This process would be swift. Climbers would wait outside the blue shelter until they were absolutely ready to release, for what lay inside was surely from the bowels of Beelzebub himself. The smell was rotten, absolutely putrid. Any longer than five minutes in there and your eyes would start to stream, your nostrils rebel. Beyond six minutes, and the active, predatory flies would rise en masse from the pit under the wooden planks and start trying to feed before their supper had been released from the unsuspecting donor. It was horrid, plain horrid. Nobody ever lingered there to read the daily papers.

Altitude does odd things to the body. Oxygen deprivation occurs noticeably above six thousand feet, producing an aching in the muscle tissues and a streaming cold similar to a mild influenza. As altitude is gained, breathing becomes more rapid, as the muscles scream for the oxygen attention they crave and deserve. Exercise and breathing feels constrained, as if you have a plastic bag over your head. The body slowly adjusts to its foreign environment by making more red blood cells to carry what little oxygen it can extract from the air breathed in, thus assisting the deprived muscles. Sleep becomes erratic, the body lapsing into a cycle driven by the build-up of carbon dioxide. Tent partners can often observe their fellow climbers apparently pausing in their breathing for up to twenty seconds or so, only to resume with a deep gasp of an inhalation when sufficient carbon dioxide has built up in the body to drive the brain's respiratory centre to take in another breath. This can, of course, cause concern if the process is not understood by the frantic observer, who can be forgiven for thinking his partner is going to die every twenty seconds. Eating becomes more difficult. The body struggles to digest most foodstuffs as altitude increases, preferring instead to produce nausea, repulsion of anything made available, and corresponding constipation from consuming a low-fibre diet. 'You've gotta put fuel in the furnace' came the frequent reminder from Tucker, our lead guide, referring to the fact that if you don't eat you won't have the energy to fuel the muscles to climb.

Day fifteen, and Tucker asked me to take a look at the assistant guide, who had become increasingly bothered with breathlessness during our ascent. Of course, at the higher altitude it is not unusual to see someone struggling a little more with their breathing. However, our assistant guide was strong and experienced, accustomed to these altitudes and normally fine with his acclimatisation strategy. We were now at nineteen thousand feet, not a place to take any chances. While both guides knew some general wilderness medicine, it seemed sensible for me to oversee the situation, as I'd developed an interest in high-altitude medicine prior to my departure, in case I was called upon to examine myself or others running into difficulty. A swift stethoscopic examination told me all I needed to know: the assistant guide had pulmonary oedema – fluid in both lungs – and so needed to descend. He was able to walk unassisted and another member of the team, deciding he'd climbed high enough, offered to escort the patient back down to base camp. Descent was the only option in that situation, and Tucker was happy to continue supervision with the now reduced group. We were now down to just six in number, including our guide. Poor weather was closing in according to the forecast, and our summit day was planned for the following morning. Everyone was to be out of their tents, packed up and ready to climb, by 5am. I was cold, tired, hungry and nervous, and felt completely unprepared for the following day's summit attempt.

I awoke abruptly after what seemed like a deep sleep to realise that only eighteen minutes had passed since my last clock check. 'Whatever happens' I thought to myself 'I must be ready on time'. The stress of being the last man out of camp is well documented and I did not want to be that person, rushing to do my final packing, forgetting to fill my water bottles, not achieving a creditable bowel movement in time before we set off. I drifted back into a restless sleep. My next abrupt awakening was slightly different: it was 5am! Tucker was shouting outside my tent, 'We leave in five minutes Alistair, don't forget to melt water for your bottles.' Damn! I could hear the other four team members outside their tents, clearly ready for departure, idly chatting, completely unaware of the blind panic taking place inside my tent. Where the heck is my head torch? Where? Oh, there on my head. Where are my spare batteries? Where's my stove, I need water, I need breakfast. It was all a disaster. I exited my tent, sat on the freezing snow, struggled to tie my crampons, my gloveless fingers freezing to the point of stinging numbness. We left for the summit, I was last out of camp, partially packed and stressed beyond my worst nightmare. 'Right, Sutcliffe'

I muttered angrily to myself into the howling, tear-inducing wind, 'that is the only time you will EVER be last out of camp.' More was to be made of this declaration later.

I trundled indignantly out of high camp, at the back of the pack, embarrassed by my inability to be ready on time for my first high-altitude summit attempt. My self-pity soon turned to excitement, as the sun started to rise and the biting winds lessened. The frosted balaclava that had warmed my inhaled breath for the last few hours became cumbersome. The alpine glow of the sunrise on the Andes backdrop to our amphitheatre drew my attention from the weariness of the climb. Suddenly it was all making sense. This was why I had come to Aconcagua. This was what I had wanted to feel. Space, awareness of every noise that dare break the sound of my crampons piercing the frozen ice beneath my feet, solitude, self-reliance and accomplishment, all producing a fulfilling comfort in my inner body. By noon we were only a couple of hours from the summit. I felt alive. For the first time in many years, I actually felt alive. At over twenty-two thousand feet, climbing freely, unaided, like I'd been here before. All senses working overtime, everything in harmony. 'I might actually get to the top of this monster.' I allowed myself to drift briefly into the land of success, until my alter ego reminded me that eighty per cent of all fatal climbing accidents occur during descent

By 2.30pm I stood atop the highest mountain I'd ever climbed, 22,835 feet up. No-one in the Western Hemisphere was above me at that moment. I felt great. All I had to do now was sign the summit register on the top, which was encased in an aluminium box for protection against the elements, take some pictures to remind me of the event, then descend safely to the steaks and beer back at base camp. The remaining team members shook hands with each other on top in a very British fashion. I felt somewhat fraudulent amongst my team, as all were more experienced than me and some had tried to climb the mountain before, yet I'd managed to succeed on my first attempt.

I had once again tasted the sweetness of success at the summit, and the many, many hours training were proving themselves worthwhile. I so wanted to share some of these moments with Clare. They were so special to me, but I knew I'd only ever be able to relay them to her through pictures and words. Both of the last two summits had left me with this pocket of sadness, but I knew and accepted that that was just the way it was.

I remember little of the descent, other than my amazement at how thick the air felt at base camp, the very same air that I'd sucked at so frantically on arrival ten days before. 'Fascinating how the body adapts,' I thought to myself. The trek back down the Vacas valley took just two days, one day less than the ascent. The remaining team members were keen to indulge in hot showers and cold coca-cola, and to take a well-earned rest.

Back at the hotel, we presented ourselves neatly at the celebration table, washed and changed, superficially resembling the people we'd been twenty days before. Beards removed, ingrained dirt scrubbed free from finger nails, skin tanned in a hit-and-miss fashion and hair bleached by the sun, we shared our final meal jovially and recounted our success to each other, as if rehearsing the stories we would tell our loved ones at home. Sweet Chilean red complemented the seared Argentinean steaks well, though my heavily cracked lips cursed the salted steak, and my mouth and tongue, burned from heavy laboured breathing up high, tried desperately to reject this now unfamiliar form of nutrition.

Arriving home from an expedition never ceases to get me excited. As I step into the arrival lounge, Clare, my long-suffering wife is always there to greet me. Slightly awkward discussion for the first few minutes, these unfamiliar people soon regain confidence in each other, and chat away as if never parted. Home felt strangely unfamiliar as we drove up the driveway. The grass in the paddock a little longer than when I left, the trees now leafless, demonstrating that winter had arrived at Moor Lodge, and the ground thick with mud from our two border collies chasing each other and anything else that moved.

Shep and Newman were our two dogs in 2003, when I summitted Aconcagua. Shep was nine and Newman was five. Shep had been a rescue dog brought down from Aberdeen to North Yorkshire. A canny, black and white border collie with an insatiable appetite, he doted on me. He slept by the side of me on our bed, always had a ball of some description in his mouth, and constantly followed me everywhere on the chance that I may, just may, stop and throw his ball for him. He used to sulk persistently when I went out, and knew when my duffel bags came down from upstairs that I was going away again. He was not averse to climbing into the larger of the two bags and lying inside it, breathing heavily and huffing to himself, demonstrating his dissatisfaction at my imminent departure and waiting in the vain hope that I might not notice a 25 kg dog in there and take him with me. Newman was a different character altogether. An agile red merle collie, he was Clare's dog, rarely venturing to me for a pat but preferring to wait by Clare for the morsel of food that would all too frequently find its way from her dinner plate and into his mouth.

Arriving back from Aconcagua was uneventful. Both dogs in prolonged contempt of me. The initial tail-wagging and licking frenzy was soon overtaken by ignoring me and rejecting my attempts at reconciliation, unless, of course, there was food attached to it. Shep was always the first of the two dogs to buckle and seek my attention again. His particular delight was my climbing jacket, ingrained with all sorts of mountain food that hadn't quite made it to its destination, instead spilling onto the front, creating the perfect snack for Shep as the jacket came out of the duffel and rested on the stone floor. Clare had overseen critical issues in the house, along with Elaine, our long-standing housekeeper and by now a close friend and confidante. The changing of a few light bulbs, opening the unpaid bills that were stacked carefully on the side for me, and life had returned to normality. A few days later it was as if I hadn't been away. Back to my medical practice, wading through three weeks' paperwork, catching up with all of the patients that had thoughtfully waited to see me instead of delivering their burdens to one of my partners, and I soon wondered if the Andes had been a dream, albeit a fantastic one. Any hardships are soon forgotten, and all the memories of the cold, the drab diet, the lack of a warm toilet seat and no hot water soon disappear. Instead, they are replaced by recounting the incredible views of ice-tipped megaliths, stone echoing in harmony with your footsteps at early dawn. Watching the sunrise through valleys of low cloud and blue sky, all pointing to the challenge that was an intimidating summit. 'So what happens now?' I thought to myself. 'Is that it?' For Clare and the dogs, the obvious answer should have been yes, but the story in my head had just started to unfold. The climb to that altitude had made me feel alive once more. I wanted to feel it again, but where to?

CLARE

Suddenly I found myself married to a mountaineer! Every inch of our spare bedroom was covered in climbing kit and all conversations were about ropes, boots, jackets and silk underwear. On one level, I was glad that Ali had a fulfilling hobby, as I was away so much from home with work. It was better than him finding another woman! On another level, I was frustrated. I was fully aware of the dangers involved, as we had in the house every 'death and disaster on mountains' book that had ever been written. I also felt envious of all the time, energy and money he was devoting to his passion and I was not able to fully share this part of his life. When I had a weekend off, he would be doing extra shifts to pay for his expedition. I understood the commitment that this needed, but sometimes, just sometimes, all a person wants in life is a change of colour in the bathroom! Our downstairs bathroom had a rancid avocado suite, which I had utterly hated from the day we moved in. Despite my many comments, Alistair's ears were deaf to the concept of a change in colour, as the cost might involve him being without a new tent, or some such item. Now, I fully appreciated the need for a cover over your head in the mountains, but avocado, and fifteen-year-old avocado for that matter! Was I really asking too much? Most of his annual leave was taken up and I spent my holidays with my sister Bernie and her husband Gil. Although I had some great vacations, it is never the same as sharing the experiences with your partner. The logistical nightmare of ensuring the dogs were looked after when he was away and I was on-call was one of my greatest challenges.

I had never spoken openly to Ali about my feelings. I wanted to be there for him and support him on his trip and wished him to leave home with no concerns about our relationship or the daily running of the house. I can count on one hand the number of arguments we have had during our time together, as both of us hate confrontation and like a steady home life. I can't remember what set us off the night before Ali went to South America, but all my frustrations came flooding out. What would happen if he got injured, or, God forbid, died during the climb? Had he ever thought what effect this would have on his family and me? Was he aware that he was so focussed on the expedition that he had almost excluded everything else from his life? Ali could not answer these questions, but just having my thoughts out in the open was comforting. I was angry with myself, however, for losing control and letting all this out the night before his trip. My timing could not have been worse and I felt guilty the whole time he was away. I would never have forgiven myself if something bad had happened to him and was relieved to see him come home in one piece. I had no idea at this point that there was a mountaineering challenge called the Seven Summits!

Chapter 3
Vinson

Antarctica, the world's last true wilderness, and Mount Vinson, the continent's highest mountain, were to be my next expedition. I had been impressed with IMG, and had decided to approach them about a place on their expedition to the frozen landscapes of this remotest of destinations. After a brief discussion with the leader of the upcoming expedition, Phil Ershler, it was agreed that I could be a member of the team. Mount Vinson stands 16,860 feet above sea level and lies in the Ellsworth mountain range. Gaining access to the mountain is something of a logistical nightmare, but the expedition to this frozen wasteland was to be the 'trip of a lifetime', I eagerly explained to my hesitant wife. Of course I'd be safe; after all, there's no disease over there. And that was it, the scene was set; I'd fly out in January of 2004, and I'd be away for three weeks, give or take a month or two!

Time passed all too quickly. Once again my bags were packed, the dogs were whining, and I was leaving the house. Clare and I were, by now, becoming more pensive as another big expedition approached. Our relationship was a strong one – we'd already been through our fair share of dramas and survived intact, but we both had inner concerns when the day of departure arrived. Clare always worried that I would fall either off a mountainside, or even worse into a big crevasse. Her fear was that nobody would be able to reach me, and that I would die alone. I had, of course, already fallen down many crevasses in my climbing career, and fortunately had lived to tell the tale – though the tale had never been told in the presence of my wife. I would never discuss any of my falls or accidents within her earshot; this was information that she did not need to know. Crevasses are dark, lonely places. The unfortunate victim would often wedge into the narrowing gap in the ice, and sometimes try to wrestle themselves out until no further energy remained, then slowly slip into hypothermia, become confused, and drift into unconsciousness prior to death. If more fortunate they would be able to extricate themselves from the premature coffin, either by ingenuity or luck and some help from other team members. My concerns as we parted were more practical. I hoped that the washing machine wouldn't malfunction, that the dogs wouldn't misbehave, or, indeed, that Clare wouldn't employ a locum to cover my position at home, looking after all departments of my 'normal' life, whilst my alter ego was away gallivanting in the mountains.

Clare took me to the airport, where we both became tearful and pledged our love for each other. Then off I went to board the plane to Santiago for the first leg of the journey to Antarctica. I must have looked odd as I got onto the plane. Due to weight restrictions imposed by airlines, and the amount of gear that climbing a mountain requires, I was always looking for ways to get a little extra weight allowance on my kit. On this occasion, I thought it wise to wear some of my high altitude climbing clothing onto the plane, namely my knee-high boots rated to minus 60 degrees Celsius, my down jacket, my insulated down trousers, and fleece hoodie. All would look normal if exiting a dome tent in the snow at 20,000 feet, but boarding a Boeing 747 and heading to my economy seat at the back of the plane, it must have looked a little strange. The flight was delayed on take-off, and landed late in Santiago. This unfortunately meant running for twenty minutes to catch my connecting flight to Punta Arenas. Running through Santiago airport fully dressed for sub-zero temperatures proved to be one of the less sensible weight-saving choices I've made in life. Arriving at Departures, sweating profusely and begging the check-in desk stewardess to kindly show mercy and let me on the connecting flight, I must have appeared comical to my new climbing team who were, unbeknown to me at the time, watching me and laughing on the other side of the departure gates. Fortunately the stewardess took pity, allowed me through, and I was soon sitting in a pool of sweat on the plane bound for the bottom of South America.

On arrival in Punta Arenas, still unaware that my climbing team were on the same flight further forward on the plane, I waited nervously for my two kit bags, without which the climb would be over before it had started. Only one bag arrived and, frustrated, I turned away from the carousel in a dejected fashion, 'No problem' a bellowing voice said in an American accent from behind me, 'happens all the time in this bloody airport!' Phil, the leader of the expedition, was standing behind me, gathering his kit bags. 'C'mon,' he said sympathetically, 'let's get to the hotel and come back for the other bags in the morning.' This was the reassurance I needed. My world wasn't, in fact, about to end abruptly because of the late arrival of a bag. Phil was a welcome sight. Short and stocky, he is a renowned and extremely successful mountaineer. His face wore the signs of many battles with the elements: cracked, scarred and irregular. The bridge of his nose went first one way then the next, as it travelled down from an off-centre beginning between two bushy eyebrows. It continued south to the blunted tip, before branching out to encircle two flared and equally bushy nostrils. His hands were unusually dark for a Caucasian, an indication of the many hours of high ultraviolet exposure devoid from protection in the hills. He was precise with his diction, caring not to use many words where a directive handful would suffice. His manner was one that I'd now become accustomed to with experienced guides, and I liked it. After all, the places that we were venturing into were potentially extremely hazardous, and I drew confidence from knowing that we were in such hands. Clearly, Phil loved the thought of returning to Antarctica. He had climbed there before and his infectious enthusiasm had me excited for the duration of the journey to the hotel. Once there, we introduced ourselves, then again settled into the now-familiar cycle of jovial discussion mixed with subtly justifying one's right to be part of the team. This time was different for me, though. I now felt strangely comfortable at meeting all these new faces and embarking on this adventure. I no longer felt the 'newbie' at this climbing game, having got lucky and seen the world from the top of Aconcagua. 'Hopefully I may be in a position to help someone out, if this is their first big expedition', I thought to myself, 'instead of being the one always asking questions and looking for assistance if any was offered.' That was, until I realized that three of the team of six had successfully climbed Denali, North America's highest peak at over twenty thousand feet, considered by many as the training ground for anyone bold enough to make an attempt on Mount Everest; the other two also had several significant summits on their curricula vitae.

The following morning Phil briefed us on the itinerary. Gear check would take place early that day, and we would fly from Punta Arenas on the first suitable weather day to Patriot Hills, Antarctica, in a chartered Russian jet. This was a six-hour flight, and completely dependent on Antarctica's weather. Crosswind speed for landing the aircraft had to be below 13 knots, otherwise the plane and our lives would be endangered. As soon as weather permitted, transfer would take place in a twin-engined Otter aircraft to Vinson base camp (7,000 feet), located 660 miles from the South Pole. The following day we would carry gear to camp 1 (9,500 feet), then descend to Vinson Base for the night. After a rest day, we would move to and set up camp 1, then take a further rest day. On day ten, we'd move to and set up camp 2 (12,500 feet), lying in the Col (valley) between Mount Shinn (the continent's second highest peak) and Vinson. Day eleven we would make our summit bid, weather permitting. By day thirteen we could be back at Patriot Hills awaiting the aircraft to return us to Punta Arenas, and home shortly after that. It all sounded so straightforward, then Phil reminded us all in no uncertain terms that this was a very unforgiving environment, and even something as minor as a broken ankle can result in death, as any help is many miles away and access remains extremely limited. We were told that they only ever took six experienced climbers on this trip, which made me feel a little uneasy, and that extensive cramponing on moderately steep slopes was the norm. Whilst the mountain had been summited by a few hundred people before us, each of them had been carefully selected by the team leader to ensure that they possessed the skill level required for the expedition. We should be able to look after ourselves in extreme conditions, and temperatures can drop to minus 40 degrees Celsius or below. Competence in glacial travel and crevasse awareness were essential requirements.

The next two days were spent getting woken at odd hours of the night being told to be on standby as the weather looked stable enough to fly to the ice, or sight-seeing around Punta after being informed that conditions had changed and that we would not be flying that day. The more anxious amongst us started discussing projected calculations of when would be the last day they could return to work without getting fired, resigning themselves to pessimistic thoughts that the weather may never let us over to the ice.

Day six saw the team boarding the enormous aircraft to take off to the explorer's last frontier. The climate on Vinson is generally controlled by the polar ice cap's high-pressure system. Conditions are predominantly stable but, as in any arctic climate, high winds and some snowfall are a possibility. There are twenty-four hours of sunlight in the summer season, November to January, and the average temperature is minus 20 degrees Celsius. Consequently, we were to have our down jackets and sunglasses to hand, along with our climbing boots for when we exited the plane onto the frozen landscape. Conditions on the six-hour, $12,000 flight were Spartan: a ham sandwich self-made mid-flight, and a canvas seat to buckle yourself into. My main concern was the fuel supply: if we were told after four hours that the winds in Patriot Hills were too strong to land, we would not have enough fuel to return to Punta Arenas. I felt sure we were all having this thought, though no-one openly discussed it.

'This is the point of no return', announced the pilot with a wry chuckle. We were half way to the white continent and couldn't turn back now as fuel reserves wouldn't allow it, 'but the weather on the ice is perfect' came the monologue, with just enough delay from the first statement to have us all clenching our buttocks. Looking through the small window, I could see nothing but ice caps, wilderness, bare rock and mountain faces. It was truly awe-inspiring: an ice desert offering the opportunity to experience an environment that few are fortunate enough to touch. But get it wrong and there would be no forgiveness.

The approach to Patriot Hills was breathtaking, with pristine peaks piercing the deep crystal blue sky. I kept pinpointing places where I could be almost certain that no living person had ever set foot. This sent a shiver down my spine, followed by a slow-rolling solitary bead of cold sweat. We really were in the middle of nowhere, miles and miles from anything one could call habitation. This, for me, had already marked out Antarctica as a very special place indeed. The plane landed almost in silence, with no back thrust from the engines as this would cause uncontrollable skidding on the ice runway, and glided to an inelegant halt some way from the large, tubular blue dome tents that were now in view. Patriot Hills houses people from across the globe. Scientists, explorers, climbers, support teams and other eccentrics gather here, in some cases for twelve months of the year, to carry out their tasks. 'Sunglasses on, hats on, boots on and down jackets on' roared Phil from his position on top of the kit bags. This was his world and things would be done his way, much to the relief of the team. We all welcomed guidance in this foreign environment.

We left the plane in single file and made our way towards the domes, clutching our kit bags. This land was unparalleled in its beauty. All I could see in every direction were peaks and plateaux. In the distance, a few ant-like figures went about their daily tasks, scurrying from one tent to another. It was warm for this time of year, about minus 5 Celsius, which made for a pleasant kit drag to the tents. This place fascinated me, from the second my feet touched down. The air smelt odd: clean, almost too clean – sterile. It reminded me of the smell inside a dentist's consulting room, giving the impression that disease was not a significant consideration here. Virtually everything was white, but no fresh snow had fallen for days. Instead, the landscape had shaped and reshaped itself with blasts of multidirectional winds. ' Landscape recognition would be difficult here', I thought to myself. 'Get lost here, and it would be the last time that you did'.

Once at the tents, we were busily hustled together by Phil for an itinerary update and a stew that had been prepared for us by some of the cooks on site. The Ellsworth mountain range, which rises from the Ronne Ice Shelf, has to be reached by small Twin Otter planes. 'They will fly us out when they are ready, not when you are ready', said Phil, 'so be on your guard for any announcements.' I knew of Phil prior to this climb. With several great summits under his belt, including Everest, he was well known as a solid decision-maker. He had previously turned back within a few hundred metres of the summit of K2, arguably the world's toughest climb, due to bad weather. His philosophy of 'ascent is optional, descent is mandatory' was a sound one. I trusted him completely to make the right calls in this most hostile of environments. 'Pick your sledges up, eat your stew, and be ready for the call.' I did as I was told, then plastered my face with sunscreen and checked my kit through once more. The latter was more for reassurance than anything else; after all, where was I going to get spare or replacement kit when we were two thousand miles from the nearest shop?

Evening soon came, determined only by the passage of time rather than sunset. At 9pm the sky was as bright as when we had landed on the ice at 1. 'Plane's ready boys, we're flying to Vinson' came the call. We'd been lucky, you can often wait for several days at Patriot Hills to leave for Vinson. We didn't need to be summoned twice. Within twenty minutes the team was arranged in the Twin Otter and the propellers were turning hungrily, eager to get airborne. Two planes waited to take us out into the Ellsworth Range, and we were informed that only one would be available for the return journey from the mountain, requiring two trips for the plane. The flight to Vinson was a fantasy of rolling ice hills, peaks and gullies, cracks in the ice and cold black rock faces, all surrounded by a penetrating blue-purple sky. I'd never seen such beauty; this really was the world's last true wilderness. Soon we arrived at our base camp (7,000 feet), located at the lower part of the Branscomb Glacier, on the west side of the Ellsworth Mountain Range. The plane was taking us further and further away from any civilisation. A mistake here, just one moment's lapse of concentration, a tired foot on the side of the mountain, would almost certainly be disastrous.

On leaving the plane, I was greeted by a base camp like no other I had been to. There was nothing here, nothing at all. No makeshift toilets, no tents, no flags, no rubbish, nothing. Completely barren. 'This'll do,' announced Phil authoritatively, pointing to a large patch of reasonably flat ice. 'We'll put up camp here'. We waved the Otter off on its return trip to Patriot Hills, and that was it, we were alone, completely. Methodically we unpacked the tents, me slower than the rest of the team, as I couldn't remember how to erect this type, despite being shown three times back in Punta. Eventually mine was up, with a little help from one of the others, and we fell into our new homes for some well-earned rest, as it was now 1am. An hour into fitful rest, the silence was shattered by a ferocious 'crack' under my head. I leapt from my sleeping bag in a cold panic and fumbled for my tent zip to see what catastrophic event was taking place. 'Relax everyone', bellowed Phil, 'it's only the ice moving, probably a few hundred miles from here. The sound gets transmitted under you.' I crept back into my hideaway, embarrassed and hoping that no-one had spotted my frantic attempt to escape the non-disaster. A few hours later and our tents were being shaken, announcing it was time to get up. We had had time to erect a makeshift lavatory – a necessity prior to any prospective climbing day. The construction of a suitable hole in the ice always takes a certain priority when camp is set up. The toilet facilities on Aconcagua were truly memorable for all the wrong reasons. But here, in this untouched landscape of utter beauty, the contrast could not have been greater. We made a simple affair, using a saw blade to cut several blocks of ice from the frozen earth, and placing them in a square, omitting just one of the sides. On the base we placed a plastic bag, ensuring that all evacuated material would be caught, so we could remove it from the camp and dispose of it appropriately back at Patriot Hills. That in itself is nothing exceptional, but where we placed the rest-room was. We erected it at the top of a small slope, providing the occupier with a view extending over miles and miles of untouched Antarctic beauty. Five minutes deliberating had been the maximum tolerated time while resting on Aconcagua, but here, well, I could have sat there all day.

I felt as if I hadn't even closed my eyes. 'This twenty-four-hour daylight thing might prove to be a nuisance,' I thought to myself. 'Tonight I'll try turning my balaclava back to front. Ingenious, that'll work for sure.' We gathered in our makeshift mess tent for some coffee and cereals, stuffed our pockets with granola bars and packets of raisins, and packed our sledges. I'd spent weeks at home preparing for this moment. During the dark early mornings in Whitby, patients from my practice had often spotted me dragging a contraption fashioned from rope and old car tyres up and down the hills on the roads near home. Most people who saw me were concerned for my sanity, but I knew that this training should hold me in good stead for pulling sledges in Antarctica. And indeed it did. We had about 30kg of weight in the small sledges that we were towing, and about the same, maybe less, on our backs. Initially the pace to camp 1 was irritatingly slow. We were all roped together, person to sledge to person, in one long line, facilitating glacier travel, the purpose being if one of us were to fall into a crevasse, then the others could aid their escape from the icy prison. Amazingly, I was not the first to find a small crevasse. A yelp from the climber directly following me indicated he'd found something that he'd not been looking for. I turned round to see Mike thigh-deep in a hole in the ice. Sheer panic helped him exit. A little thrashing around on the surface and within a couple of minutes, before I could reach him, he was clear. Rather dishevelled, he soon regained his composure and we were off once again, pulling through the virgin snow towards what was to be our camp 1, six miles and 2,100 feet further up the hill.

Six hours later we arrived. It was yet another deserted plateau. The routine was set, we unpacked, erected the tents, sorted out the 'posh' – which was our term for the mess tent – and set about getting some food. John, also from the UK, was a team member with whom I got on well. A tall, tanned gent, who lived in the UK for most of the year, and the rest of the time in his apartment in Chamonix. A keen skier and climber, John had previously spent time in Antarctica on a land expedition retracing some of Shackleton's steps. He had a London accent, and appeared to be from a wealthy background. At over six foot tall and broad-shouldered, I felt sure he would prove to be a strong member of the team. He was good fun, telling comical tales of situations back home, frequently making us all chuckle. He was to be my tent companion for the rest of the trip, and that worked well. Most of my tent etiquette I learned from John, and it has been of benefit since. He was a thoughtful chap, the only member to bring a small brush on the expedition to remove excess snow from his clothing before coming into the tent. There was another John on the trip, a reserved and quiet American, very pleasant and friendly, who I would meet again on a future trip to Everest. The remaining two were also Americans: Mike, who worked in the banking industry I believe, and Steve, a six feet six inch aspiring actor and part-time pilot. By the end of our short outward stay at camp 1, we were all on familiar terms with each other. This was a good team and I felt comfortable in their company.

The journey to camp 2 was similar to that which took us to camp 1. Sledge-pulling, resting, drinking, groaning at the sledges, tripping over the ropes and occasionally falling indignantly to the ground, having caught the crampon points from one foot on the upper part of the boot on the other foot. Once at camp 2 having got ourselves in order, we were instructed in the art of ice-wall building. 'It can get windy at this point', explained Phil. 'Gather round and I'll show you how to build a wall'. He energetically cut through the ice with a small, serrated blade, to form blocks, then placed them side by side and on top of each other. We all picked up our blades and followed suit. Eventually a decent wall had been built surrounding our tents, providing good protection from the prevailing winds.

Steve called me over to his tent. He was sitting on his roll mat, right boot off, inspecting his toes in a worried fashion. I went over to take a look. It was a mess: fungal infection, blisters and sores. It turned out he'd brought boots one size too small. I helped him with some dressings. The climb to camp 3 was a fixed line section, which involves climbing with the assistance of a line in place, held into the ice by spikes. The elevation gain was roughly 1,500 feet, and took several hours. Each climber attached himself to the rope via an ascender, a device fastened to the harness and clipped into the rope with teeth angled in one direction. This allows unidirectional travel up a rope, locking into place after each haul and thus prevents the climber slipping back down. The slope requires crampons and ice axe as well to climb it. These fixed lines need regular maintenance, and this section was the crux of climbing Vinson. I was nervous about it. I had never been up fixed lines before, or used an ascender. Slow and secure would be my motto.

Our first attempt at making headway up to camp 3 was soon thwarted by bad weather. Another team, who'd set up their camp 2 nearby, foolishly decided to proceed up the fixed lines, resulting in some uncomfortable frostbite to one of their member's fingers. Smug in the knowledge that Phil had turned us round before the wind had picked up, I felt sure he'd make the right call on the time to ascend these lines. This was indeed the case. The following day, after a meal of eggs, bread, cereal and hot drinks, we set out and reached the base of the fixed lines. I knew if I was to a) summit Vinson, and b) continue climbing more difficult mountains, I'd need to master the ascending and descending technique quickly and with precision. I listened intently as Phil expertly showed us how to use our tools, and up we went. The technique soon became obvious. Don't use your arms to pull, instead use your legs to push. The leg muscles are far bigger than the arm muscles, and tire much more slowly. Soon I was hauling myself up the line with relative ease. It was fun, it was something new, and I'd learnt how to do it, and that is always rewarding. Tired but satisfied, the team pulled into camp 3. This was to be our last camp before the summit. Now at 12,300 feet, the air felt thinner. Being polar, it feels more like 16,000 feet had it been in an equatorial position, as the air is more rarefied at the poles due to the rotation of the earth. Camp 3 was situated in a broad col between Vinson and Shinn, the continent's second highest peak, and magnificent in its stature. The views were incredible, a virgin landscape of ice mountains and snow-covered terrain as far as the eye could see. Phil told us that we'd have a rest day the following day, to help with acclimatisation, then summit day would be long, between twelve and fourteen hours.

That first night at camp 3 was the coldest that I'd ever experienced. Vicious winds pushed the temperature down to minus 60. I had almost all of my climbing clothing on inside my down sleeping bag, along with two balaclavas, two hats, and three pairs of gloves. I was still cold. Eventually, I had to get out of my sleeping bag and exercise inside my tent to warm up my core, and then retreat back to my sleeping bag in a vain attempt to retain some of the heat that I'd generated. The following night, after a lazy day of playing cards, drinking and resting, supper wasn't easy. A couple of team members were having trouble eating – altitude often does this. The food tastes different as the body is more interested in sending blood to its core structures – brain, heart and lungs – than it is to the digestive system. I've never had a problem eating at altitude, remembering Tucker's adage of 'gotta put fuel in the furnace'. I found that if I didn't think about what I was eating but just got on and ate it quickly, my body didn't get time to reject it. It worked for me. The average weight loss by the team members on Aconcagua had been ten pounds; I'd put on two pounds. This trip would probably be similar. The evening was spent quietly, team members obviously contemplating the big summit push the following day. By now I'd become accustomed to the twenty-four-hour daylight and consequently was resting a little easier. 'We'll leave at 8am,' announced Phil. 'I don't want any stragglers, be ready'. I didn't know if this was directed at me, but inside I felt as if it was. After all, I was the one that had been the straggler on Aconcagua; I felt sure Phil must have heard this on the grapevine.

The next morning I was up at 5.30am, and ready for the summit. Of course, no-one else had even stirred yet, but that was not the point. I would be ready, fully packed, water in my bottles, and raring to go. I would not be the 'last man out' this time. I felt self-righteous.

The summit climb was spectacular, the final summit ridge consisting of an unforgettable rock and ice traverse. From the summit we were blessed with fine weather, giving glorious views of neighbouring Mount Shinn and Mount Gardner, along with a multitude of unexplored peaks. Wow! I'd made it to the summit of the highest mountain in Antarctica, and I felt great. As far as the eye could see, nothing but snow and ice, no signs of civilisation or previous human interference. It was perfect. This was my idea of wilderness. On the horizon, some two hundred miles or so in the distance, a grey-blue fuzz merged seamlessly into a thin grey pencil-line, designating the point where sky and land held hands in the rarefied atmosphere. What a privilege to experience this beauty. We had felt the wrath of the Antarctic katabatic winds at camps lower down, but not today. The air at the top tasted peculiar. It had an empty quality – no flavours from low valley trees, no pollution from far away suburbs, not even an interruption from the occasional icy winds that we'd experienced. Today, the Gods had granted us safe passage to the summit and granted us permission to savour it in all of its true and natural beauty. The summit was small, less than two feet or so across, just enough space for a couple of us to stand together at any one moment. We congratulated ourselves, eagerly shaking each other's hands and hugging.

I made a point of thanking Phil, as without his guidance I would not have had the skills to reach this point. I pulled out my satellite phone and broke the good news to Clare. She was relieved, and reminded me that my cousin Shelley was getting married in three days, and I should ring them on their wedding day if I could. I phoned my parents too, then let some of the other team members phone their loved ones, and soon it was time to retreat down the mountain.

The descent to base camp was straightforward. Back at base camp, the can of beer that I'd taken over to the white continent to celebrate any success on the climb had frozen solid, much to the disappointment of my sunburned mouth and tongue. Amazingly, the Otter planes were at base camp dropping off some other climbers, so we hitched a ride directly back to Patriot Hills. There our luck continued, as the Russian jet was restocking. The weather was perfect for a return flight, so we were quickly gathered and bustled onto the jet. Six hours later, and we were back at Punta Arenas. Without waiting, I went straight to the LAN Chile airline office and asked about flight status for a trip to Santiago. Remarkably, two places were left on the flight due to leave in three hours. John and I booked our seats, returned to the hotel, said our goodbyes and headed for the airport. Unbeknown to us, it was a bank holiday in Punta. Our flight was the last available for three days, so the others remained marooned at the hotel until then. From Santiago, I caught a flight the following day, then the train from London to York, where I got a taxi to a small hotel 25 miles away. This was the hotel at which my cousin and her husband were having their wedding reception. I'd made it. Unwashed, bearded, and only a quick change of clothing, but miraculously I'd made it. From the top of the highest mountain in Antarctica to a wedding reception outside York in two and a half days: it must have been a record. Clare's eyes greeted me from her table at the reception, though she didn't initially realise that it was her husband. A few seconds later, she looked back at me in disbelief and exclaimed that I was there. I think it was a bit of an interruption in the speeches, but the reception went well. I shared stories with some of my family who were there, and congratulated the newly married couple. Antarctica was over, and I had returned to normality. It had been a truly unforgettable climb, my favourite so far.

CLARE

Of all of Ali's expeditions, I would have loved to go to Antarctica. The timing and cost of this was prohibitive, but he has promised to take me there someday. Ali regularly gives public talks to raise money for a local hospice and his descriptions and pictures of this vast continent are always one of the highlights for me. It is a truly desolate, quiet place.

I had come to terms with my role of mountaineer's wife and tried to keep life as normal and busy as possible when he was away. He managed to call me on the satellite phone every few days, but we never arranged a formal time in case he could not get a signal and I started to worry that something had gone wrong. Bad news always travels quickly in the mountaineering world and we all live by the motto 'no news is good news'. I knew that on most climbing parties, tragedy was an unwelcome, but expected visitor. Ali and I had an unspoken rule that he did not tell me of any accidents or fatalities on the trip until he was home and, even then, he kept the details to a minimum. Although the risks of climbing were real, I never really believed that anything untoward would happen to Ali. He had always been a lucky person, so I didn't think about it. I just got up every day, walked the dogs, went to work and came home. Routine is a great way to avoid the feelings of loneliness and depression.

I was delighted that he made it back in time for Shelley's wedding, as I hate going to formal occasions without a partner. He appeared at the entrance of the hotel with a full beard and wearing clothes that had not been washed for a month! I marched him straight up the stairs to our room and put him in the bath. After half an hour, he smelt considerably better and almost resembled my husband again. The reception was a great success and we spent a fabulous weekend getting to know each other again before returning home to Whitby.

Chapter 4
Denali

The spring of 2004 saw the untimely death of Newman, our young border collie. He had gone over some cliffs near where we live whilst chasing something. I'd managed to rescue him from the cliff ledge and got him to the vet, but after five days and several operations, he unfortunately succumbed to his injuries. We buried him in our garden and said a prayer for him, amongst our tears and consoling whiskies. My father had always said that when one dog passes on another should be brought into the home, to relieve the sorrow and bring company for the other dog, and once again he was proved right. Chino was another border collie, from the same breeder as Newman, and was seemingly destined to be with us. On Newman's untimely passing, I had searched all the local ads to try to find his breeder, but she had moved and changed phone numbers. In despair, I picked up a copy of the Yorkshire Post, flicked to the adverts, spied one saying 'border collie pups for sale' and phoned up. To my utter amazement, Michelle answered. She had been Newman's breeder and the lady I'd been searching for. I recounted his tragedy, and enquired on the off chance whether she had any puppies ready now. She had, and gave us first refusal. Over we went that day, and back with us came Chino, our new brown and white beautiful baby. Shep, our rescue collie, was not amused at having to put up with another puppy. Chino, on the other hand, was delighted to have another dog's ears to chew and a tail to hang from.

April 2004 was a milestone in my best friend Steve's life. He'd suffered a heart attack several years before when serving on the submarines. He'd now given up smoking, and had trained to run a full marathon. As we went over the finishing line of the Paris Marathon together, I felt honoured to have shared the moment, for it obviously meant a great deal to him. Home duties, family illness and increasing workload at the medical practice curtailed climbing for the remainder of 2004, but early 2005 saw me trawling through my climbing books once more. 'I've been high and I've been cold,' I thought to myself. 'Now it's time to go both high and cold. Denali was the obvious choice. A massive and impressive pyramid of stone, it is a mountain that needs no explanation as to why it should be climbed. It has a magnetism that continually draws climbers from around the world. It never gives up its summit easily, and success truly confirms the eager climber as a mountaineer. It stands at 20,320 feet and is the highest mountain in North America. It is considered America's most classic climb, rising 18,000 feet in elevation from bottom to top, the highest elevation gain in the world. At northern latitude of 63 degrees, it is the most northerly mountain over 20,000 feet. The giant Alaskan range is reached by small planes setting out from near Anchorage. I felt ready for Denali (also called McKinley, after a presidential candidate in the 1800s). I continued training hard and in my mind pitched Denali as a hard Vinson. More sledge-pulling, more fixed lines, extremes of temperatures, and three weeks from home. Careful discussion with Clare, Shep and Chino secured approval, sealed with many trips to the florist for Clare and to the butchers for the dogs. I trained well, continuing my regime of long-distance running, aiming to complete a marathon every eight weeks or so, and sledge pulling. By now, my neighbours and patients were used to seeing me pulling my tyres up the hills, and thought nothing of driving past me to offer encouragement and cakes on occasion. That is Whitby – everybody knows what everybody else is up to, most are related, and, in general, they all care about those in their vicinity. It is a great place to live.

Early June 2005 saw me leave the house once more to undertake a climb. This time was different, though. I knew it would be tough, I knew success rates were much lower than on Aconcagua and on Vinson, and I also knew that I only had three weeks, as the summer is a very busy time at work. The day before departure had been spent with our closest friends Steve and Lou and their charming daughters Hel and Cas. We'd known them since moving to Whitby. Steve was a local doctor at a neighbouring practice, who also shared a love of motorbikes. An ex-submarine naval doctor, he had come out of the navy after twelve years and moved into family medicine. We'd met on the steps of the local hospital: Steve, somewhat vertically challenged yet stocky, good looking in a fatherly friendly type of way, sucking on a cigarette, his leg in plaster from a recent accident, was sitting by the motorcycle that he'd ridden up to the hospital on his day off. I knew we'd hit it off even before we spoke to each other, and I was right. We have discovered over the years that we share many loves in common; fine wine, motorcycling, long-distance running, and of course, we both showed excellent taste in our choice of wives; Clare and Lou who were like best friends from day one.

Leaving for the airport with Clare, I felt a strange sense of foreboding. I knew that this climb would be harder than the previous ones, and that success was much less likely, but also had a deep inner feeling that we would be faced with increasingly difficult decisions and danger would present itself more frequently and in greater magnitude. I don't know why I felt this way. I'd always had some apprehension as Clare and I parted at airport check-in terminals, but I hadn't felt like this before. I'm sure that Clare sensed my unease, but she tactfully chose to avoid mentioning it in our final exchanges of words and hugs.

My flight was from London to Anchorage, then on to Talkeetna. I met the other members of the team there, including James and Nick who I already knew from a weekend climbing in Wales. I had a strong feeling that with both of them on the climb, we'd enjoy a successful time. We all met up in Talkeetna and those who were unfamiliar with the others quickly got acquainted. It seemed like a strong team of ten, including two guides. We would essentially climb as one party, but have two internal teams. The senior guide, Ryan, would be leading my team, and Nick and James would be two of the other three climbing with us, which suited us perfectly. Following the mandatory kit-check at the nearby hotel, Ryan outlined the itinerary. We would fly aboard the ski-equipped aircraft to base camp on the south-east fork of the Kahiltna Glacier at 7,300 feet. From there we'd move to camp 1 (7,900 feet), then onto camp 2 (10,000 feet) at the Kahiltna pass, following the Kahiltna glacier. Camp 3 would be at 11,500 feet, and camp 4 at 14,200 feet. Camp 5 was reached by ascending more fixed lines, this time at 50 degrees, up to 17,300 feet. From there, we'd await a weather window to try for the summit at 20,320 feet, hopefully returning to Talkeetna within 21 days.

The hotel, unlike many of the previous ones, was delightful. Run by an eccentric overweight local lady who just loved the attention of all of the young men in her boudoir, she was an epic hostess. Her cooking was wonderful and her home was spotless, which helped to settle the team into good spirits. The first few days of any expedition are always important. It's an anxious time for all, but more so for those who aren't familiar with anyone else on the team. With 'fuel in the furnace' and good beds for rest, we soon set about our business of checking and double-checking all of the relevant equipment prior to departure for the mountain.

Denali, the Native American name for the peak, meaning 'The High One', is situated just 390 kilometres from the Arctic Circle and, standing 20,320 feet above sea level, it represents the perfect training ground for those who aspire to climb Mount Everest. Altitude sickness, frostbite, death and rescue are all par for the course on Denali. Like Vinson, it is a polar mountain, rendering climbers more hypoxic. The barometric pressure is lower for a given altitude than on mountains closer to the equator. This difference becomes noticeable above 10,000 feet, and it makes the summit of Denali equivalent to anywhere from 21,000 to 23,000 feet in the Himalaya, depending on weather conditions. Winter brings a much lower barometric pressure than in the summer. This lowered pressure means less oxygen in the air. The mountain thus produces more of a physio-logical challenge than would be expected for its altitude. There is one preferred route, that of The West Buttress. Although it is not technically difficult, one needs to plan for extreme survival situations. 70mph winds and temperatures of minus 40 are not uncommon, and rarely does the mountain pass through a season without claiming a life. 2005 was to be no exception. Some climbers dreadfully underestimate this mountain, often at their peril. Accident rates of six per cent were not uncommon on Denali, though this has been improved recently by a growing respect for the route. For those sufficiently prepared for the climb, a success rate of 50% is not unachievable, if prevailing conditions are in favour. Climbing falls are the commonest cause of fatalities (39%), followed by hypothermia (21%) crevasse falls (11%), pulmonary oedema (6%), cerebral oedema (5%), carbon monoxide poisoning (3%), and unknown (15%). Of the fatalities occurring on Denali, 44% occur on the ascent, 56% on the descent.

I began to feel Denali's magnetism on stepping out of the Beaver ski plane at base camp. The Beavers were more simple than the Otters we'd used on Vinson, but neither felt particularly safe once airborne. Denali's massive chaos of ice and rock was both mysterious and inaccessible. Its great walls and ridges easily visible, the mountain stood alone, dominating the landscape. My heart was thumping; this was going to be hard. It looked different from the other mountains I'd climbed. A perfect pyramid reflecting shards of light from its gullies, showing off its summit boldly with wisps of spindrift at the top, like fine hair on a newborn child. But this was no baby. It held many dark secrets, retaining many of the bodies that had exhaled their last breaths on its slopes, covering them with a death cloak of snow, ice and rock. This was a climb to respect.

We made base camp much like any other. Tents were eagerly erected, kit was sorted, sledges were loaded and stoves were then fired up. Talking into the dusk, Ryan went through the plans again. We would leave the following morning at 6am, to do our first carry up to camp 1.

I, of course, was up and ready by 5am. When the team was finally prepared for departure, we put on our snowshoes, attached ourselves to our sledges, and set off. The carry to camp 1 was uneventful, apart from the grunting and huffing from those who hadn't pulled sledges any distance in snow before. James, Nick and I joked our way up, recounting stories from home, and planning who'd be responsible for the first round of drinks back in Talkeetna on our successful return. Camaraderie is strong amongst mountaineers. Attached by a lifeline to each other, one small mistake, a lapse in concentration, an over-eager stride across an untested path, and it is your fellow climbers who'll be first to help save your life. It takes time to trust each other, but we had climbed together before and I felt comfortable with the three of us roped together. I was sure they felt the same. The following day we moved to camp 1 proper, creating ice walls to protect the tents from the vicious winds that whipped up without a moment's notice. After an uncomfortable night's rest at 7,900 feet, largely due to the incessant howling of the wind, and the bailing out of snow and ice that the wind forced into every nook and crack inside our tent, we headed to camp 2 (10,000 feet) on the Kahiltna Pass. Care had to be exercised, as the huge glacier field we were crossing had claimed plenty of lives in the past. The ropes between team members had to be kept reasonably taut: breaking a fall into one of these icy tombs is all the more difficult if the unfortunate body has fallen a distance first, through the rope being too slack. At camp 2, we rested for a day, and gathered our thoughts. The next part of the climb involved steeper terrain, so from now on we would be carrying all the weight on our backs, as sledges could not be used. This meant loading the rucksacks with about 70 pound loads and correct packing was essential to avoid unnecessary injury. Big loads had been carried on Aconcagua, but these were bigger. I knew this would strain my back, putting pressure on previous injury areas from motorcycle accidents and over-vigorous long-distance runs. I elected to start a course of Ibuprofen, an anti-inflammatory, in the hope of keeping injury to a minimum. Self-medicating is one of the advantages of being a doctor on an expedition. The drawbacks are all too obvious – why would the guides elect to treat a climber if there's a doc on board? I didn't really mind though, as I had an interest in high altitude medicine, and at home helped run a busy accident and emergency unit, so I felt comfortable with most things that could crop up.

The climb up to camp was hard work. My knees creaked and groaned under the strain of all the weight that I was asking them to carry, and my toes ached from constant kicking forwards in my climbing boots to ensure a safe foothold in the icy terrain. This was Denali – hard and tiring. It was proving to be just what I had expected.

The move to camp 3 (11,500 feet) went according to plan. Once there, we were treated to exquisite views of the 3,000 foot rock that lay ahead and every face on the edge of the West Buttress. The weather remained in our favour, so it was decided that we'd move to camp 4 (14,200 feet) the following day. Progress was swift, and we were way ahead of schedule – at present. We moved successfully up to camp 4 as planned, passing around Windy Corner, which exposed stunning panoramic views of surrounding peaks and the northeast fork of Kahiltna Glacier 4,000 feet below. The move to camp 5 (17,200 feet) would be the most demanding part of the climb, so a rest day at camp 4 was in order. We had made excellent progress to get this high so quickly, but as we all pulled into camp 4 we were starting to look tired. Knees and backs had suffered most from our efforts, with bursting muscles and spent joints demanding rest. James was acclimatising well, better than most of us, and I awoke the following day to the sight of him brandishing his ice axe atop a mound of snow, pointing eagerly at his creation. For the previous couple of hours, he'd been building a snow castle, some eight feet high, from carefully carved ice blocks, and it was now complete. He took off his climbing shirt, undid the fly on his black climbing pants, put his ice axe carefully down his trousers, and let the shaft of the axe exit through the open zip. 'I AM the king of the castle!' he exclaimed joyously. At which the remaining team members saw fit to start bombarding him with snowballs. After the fights, we ate crispy bacon, drank coffee, and remarked on our good fortune at getting to this altitude in such swift fashion. This rest day had come at the right time for all of us.

The following day was a hard day for me, in more ways than one. Sometimes just putting one foot in front of the other can seem such a difficult thing to do. My boots felt unusually heavy, my crampons added what seemed like a stone to the weight of each foot. The air felt sharp as I breathed it in, cutting through my airways, constricting all the passages before finally coming to rest in my starving lungs. My mouth, agape from trying to force more air into the empty zones of my lungs, was burnt inside. The snow had reflected the strong rays off the snow into the roof of the mouth and had scorched the tender flesh that housed the upper surface of my tongue. Swallowing saliva became painful, and eating became problematic, but nutrition still had to be forced in somehow. I was cold, even though we were working hard, jigging our way up the fixed lines using the methods I'd learnt on Vinson. The ropes were frozen, so I continually had to clean them with my gloved hand, otherwise the ascenders' teeth couldn't grip properly and I'd slide back to the previous anchor point. I was not in a good place, and my spirits were low. In a strange way, I was driven on from seeing two others on the team, Russ and Sam, also struggling on this move to our high camp. Some mutual banter and encouragement saw the three of us arrive exhausted into camp 5. 'God, I pray we have a rest day tomorrow', I exclaimed to them. For the first time on a climb, I was really tired. I figured it was probably a combination of the reasonably quick ascent that we had made through the camps, a couple of poor night's sleep due to raging winds after dark, and my back starting to twinge from the heavy loads we were now carrying. I kept on reminding myself that I was here by choice, and that I'd even paid for the privilege, so I should stop grumbling and get back to enjoying it. After all, what would I rather be doing, climbing this fantastic mountain in unseasonably settled conditions, or doing a busy surgery with twenty booked appointments and five extra patients at the end? The choice was an easy one, and I fired up my stove to set about refuelling my body with the energy and fluid that it now craved. I must have slept well that night, even though my body had fought for the little oxygen that existed in the atmosphere. I didn't dream, which was unusual for me, especially during periods of oxygen starvation, and I awoke refreshed and hungry at early dawn. It had clearly been a cold night, as the first movement in my tent showered tiny ice crystals from the patchwork sides and roof glistening down onto my cocooned body.

My sleeping bag took the majority of the frosted vapour, the rest finding its way onto my face and down the back of my warm neck.

'We'll try for the summit tomorrow' announced Ryan the following morning, 'weather permitting. So fill up your bellies, fill up your bladders, and enjoy the day here at 17,200 feet.' I was relieved; my body needed a rest. A short walk from my tent gave a clear view of camp 4 almost 3,000 feet below. It had been a tough climb up from that camp, and our tents appeared minuscule on the plateau below, like felt-tip pen dots on white paper. I rested well that day, and felt ready for the summit attempt, but my eagerness was in vain. That evening had witnessed a change in the weather. Further down the glacier we could see heavy clouds accompanied by high winds further up the ridge. The spindrift was flowing freely from the summit, indicating strong winds further up. It seemed unlikely that we would be going anywhere for the next few days. And so it was. After four days at high camp, all teams – ours and those around us – were becoming audibly frustrated. We'd waited for a break in the weather to try for the top, but it had not come. We'd become bored with the chess and card games, and all wanted to move on, to get the job done and get back to a few beers in Talkeetna, and home to our loved ones. We were only 3,000 feet from our goal; surely the weather wouldn't deny us now? Some of the team members understandably started making rumblings about needing to get home for work commitments. I discussed this with James and we both agreed that we'd come here to try to summit Denali and that we would wait for the weather to break, provisions and gas permitting. I discussed this with Ryan and he agreed that, if necessary, he could stay on a while with us and the assistant guide could lead down the other climbers who needed to get back. Whilst this would not be ideal, as we all shared the common goal of a successful, safe summit and descent, James and I were not under the same time constraints as the others. I had always felt confident that, if absolutely necessary, my partners at work would continue to cover for my patients if my absence had to be slightly extended.

Day 5 at high camp was a bad day. Two brothers had set off for the summit, even though the weather had not changed. Half way through the ascent, while traversing a difficult ridge, one had slipped and fallen, taking the other with him at the end of his rope. From the ridge they'd fallen 6,000 feet to their deaths. Their bodies were clearly visible though inaccessible from where we stood at high camp. I felt sick. 'Why do we do this most selfish of pursuits?' I thought to myself. It has no real gain other than self-gratification. Is it really fair to leave those that we love at home, worrying, so that we can satisfy these desires? What must the families of those brothers, now contorted and lifeless at the base of the ridge, be thinking? Cursing, no doubt, the drive that took their loved ones so prematurely from them. But then we knew the risks, though somehow they didn't apply to us. Often climbers feel invincible, at least until the day that they fall. Once again Denali had claimed life, a stark reminder that there was no room for error on the slopes of these giants.

By day seven at high camp, it was looking grim. We'd waited out the weather about as long as we could. Food was almost out, and gas was also in short supply. With no gas, there's no heat to melt snow, hence no water. 'Tomorrow is our up-down day, team', Ryan announced authoritatively. This meant that we would retreat down the mountain tomorrow if the weather did not change in our favour, as supplies were now severely limited and people needed to get back. The mood of the team was low; we all knew what that meant. I went to bed that night full of angst. Could we really be so close to the summit, 10,000 miles from home, to fail because of the weather? This would be the first time I'd turned back from the summit on a big expedition, and I wasn't looking forward to the experience. I knew Ryan didn't want to turn back either, but it was the only option. I did not relish the idea of returning to these slopes for a repeat performance. It had been a hard and draining climb, both physically and now mentally. I did not like the thought of possible failure, but understood the reasons why it was presenting itself. I knew that I'd find it much harder to return to repeat a climb where I'd previously failed, but reconciled that with the knowledge that failure due to poor weather was acceptable if that was the way that the expedition panned out.

Day eight at high camp saw an amazing change in our fortune. The wind had died down, the spindrift on the top was not visible, and the sun was rising unobstructed in a clear sky. It was 6am, and through the open zip in my tent I noticed Ryan uncoiling the ropes. That meant we were going up, as the way down had fixed lines. My heart was thumping, and I pounced on James, barely able to control myself. I shook him by the shoulders. 'Get up, big fella' I exclaimed, 'we're heading up!' I eagerly gathered things together and set about preparing myself for our assault on the summit. By 9am we were all ready. The hour I'd spent waiting for the others to get ready I'd amused myself guessing who the last man out would be today. As per usual it was James, as relaxed as ever, carefully preparing himself and not in the least bit concerned that he might be the one to get the title. James was a great friend to be around. He relaxed me, brought everything down to a realistic level, and offered help when it was needed. He was a dependable team member and I was glad this expedition had brought us together. We were advised that we would be climbing close to where the brothers had so tragically lost their lives, and to make sure that we never let our guard down. With some snowfall during the recent storm, conditions could be unpredictable. We threw our rucksacks on, roped up, and set off for the summit.

The day was a long and cold one. On the way up, we passed the now frozen, multicoloured bodies of the brothers lying close to each other, their down suits ripped open from the fall against the rock. I hoped they were still together in what lay ahead of them, their lives so tragically brought to a premature end. I said a small prayer as we passed them, and turned my concentration up to the maximum. We were not within distance to effect a body-retrieval, but the radios had informed us that the climbing rangers were taking care of this.

The route saw us traversing a steep snow face to Denali Pass. From there we followed gentle slopes to Archdeacon's Tower and a large plateau at 19,500 feet known as the Football Field. From there, we ascended moderate terrain to the crest of the summit ridge. I looked down upon the immense 8,000 feet South Face, with Cassin Ridge and the South Buttress in view. This was why I loved climbing. All the previous seven days' waiting around for decent weather evaporated into a distant memory. This was spectacular, and we were here. The last 300 feet to the summit were along a truly exposed ridge. Utmost concentration was required to avoid any careless slip. Death was almost guaranteed if the feet were not cautious here. When we reached the top, the relief was palpable. The whole team thanked Ryan and the assistant guide, and then I turned to James. 'Fancy a shot at Everest sometime?' 'Sure,' he replied, in typical laid-back fashion. 'Why not?' The views back down the climbing route to the lower camps were fantastic. The clear skies brought with them crystal visions of the surrounding snow-laden peaks, the exposed darkened faces of nearby mountains, and uninterrupted views down the giant glaciers. We'd got lucky just when we needed to, and got the break in the weather that we'd all hoped for so desperately. All storm fronts had now disappeared, the sun had risen, and we'd made the summit.

'Ascent is optional, descent is mandatory', I mantra'd to myself several times, as we turned to start our retreat. James was ahead of me this time on the rope. I'd taken a couple of caffeine energy gels on the summit, and was now ready for the descent. The sooner we got down, the sooner I could get home and see Clare and the dogs. As always I'd missed them but tried not to think of them too often, focussing my energies rather on the task in hand with the climb. Clare knew this, she'd been married to me now for long enough to know what I was like. I've never lacked focus. Once my mind is set on a task, it has to be seen through to completion, if at all possible. I'd left the satellite phone at high camp to reduce weight, but intended to phone her that evening. Along the narrow traverse on the descent I noticed that James, ahead of me, wasn't his usual buoyant self. I fixed my eyes on his footwork and noticed that it was awkward. As if I'd foreseen the next two seconds of my life, I grabbed my ice axe firmly in my right hand, then James slipped. An all-too-easy mistake, he caught his right crampon in his left lower trouser, and started falling down the ridge. Before he'd gathered any momentum, I'd thrown myself to the ground, thus arresting his fall as soon as the lifeline between us went tight. 'Thanks Ali, just checking you were awake' came the cry from the other side of the knife-edge ridge, in typical James fashion. We laughed, James joked that he needed to change his underwear, and we continued down the mountain. We all made it down in one piece, I phoned Clare from high camp, and collapsed onto my mattress. We were exhausted, but we were almost there, almost down and heading back towards reality. The rest of the hike out passed without problems, despite the enormous loads we each carried on our backs, clearing each of our camps out as we descended down the hill. My back held out, just, aided by a carefully constructed diet of energy gels and anti-inflammatory medication.

Two days later we were back in Anchorage. James, Nick and I headed out for a few celebratory beers and some food prior to flying out the following day. The others chose either to rest in the hotel or to re-schedule flights to try and return home that day. I talked with James at length that evening about the prospect of going to Everest. Eventually he decided he would probably look at it for 2007. I thought I could get time from the practice the following year, 2006. But was I really ready to try to climb the world's highest mountain? That night, before my return flight home, my mind went back to my first meeting with Chris Bonington and how excited I'd been, listening eagerly to his stories when I was 11 years old. The thoughts of wanting to see, feel, hear, smell and taste the world from its rooftop. Was it time to put those dreams into a workable plan? I thought so, but would Clare?

CLARE

I knew by this time that Ali would continue climbing until he had completed the Seven Summits, however long this took. I admired him greatly for his commitment and passion for the project, but I was starting to struggle with the consequences of Ali achieving his dream. I was working seventy miles from home and trying desperately to keep things going. Ali's dad came up to help me for a week when I was on night duty. I love that old man to bits and always enjoyed his company, but I felt obliged to be at home as much as possible and lived on just a couple of hours sleep every day. There is no doubt that high altitude mountaineering is a completely selfish occupation. When I ask Ali why he does it, he tells me that he enjoys the simplicity of life on the mountains, concentrating only on keeping warm, hydrated and nourished. Those of us left at home have to juggle every aspect of daily life and live with the uncertainty of our loved ones returning.

Mountaineers are a very varied group of people. Ali often invites climbers to visit us in Yorkshire after the expeditions finish. A few are completely egotistical and spend the evenings talking about themselves and their vast climbing experience; they wear their summit conquests like medals of honour. Others are extremely introspective and are quietly content with their achievements. James has always been my favourite. He is an extremely well-educated man who works for the Forestry Commission and just lives for the outdoors. After long days in the operating theatre and poorly air-conditioned hospital wards, I often long to have a job like James, where I could spend my days outside in the fresh air.

Chapter 5
Everest

Back home, and life soon returned to normal. Busy surgeries, nights out catching up with friends, and endless attention paid to the dogs. Following the initial excitement of their owner's return, the dogs soon settled back into the routine of ignoring me for a few days, then forgiving me when they realised that I could reach the biscuit tin and they couldn't. Clare and I talked at length about the possibility of climbing Everest. She was great in these discussions, never rejecting any of my seemingly mad plans, just busily reminding me of the death rates, the cost and the time involved. Resigned, however, she knew in her heart that I longed to go, and better I go with her blessing than without. I'd spoken to the practice about it several years before. As in any democracy, plans are best spoken about early on; approval is then gained, as the process seems like a long time ahead. Then, when the time has arrived to put the plan into action, it has already been agreed several years previously. While this fact may, of course, have been forgotten, I always make sure that such agreements get minuted from these practice meetings. We have always been supportive of each other at work, and this time was no exception. I had found a suitable locum to cover, and with the agreement of the practice, and the blessings of my wife and family, it was set. I was to go to Kathmandu in the spring of 2006, on a mission to climb Mount Everest, the highest mountain in the world, and the subject of my dreams for 31 years. I had emailed Chris Bonington to tell him of my plans, and he'd wished me success on the expedition. I was good to go.

Funding these adventures was never easy. It required many, many nights on-call, sitting in a poorly-lit, cold and lonesome room, staring at a computer screen and answering calls to patients requesting advice. It was often stressful and tiring, but did help provide the funds to go to these fantastic places. I would often be out of the house for ten or more nights a month, a sacrifice that Clare rightly questioned. This commitment would make it all the sweeter if the expedition was successful.

Training went well. It largely consisted of running 35-45 miles a week for endurance, weight training for strength, and gaining mental focus for the task that lay ahead. March 28th 2006, departure day for Kathmandu, soon came round. I said my farewells to Shep and Chino, who'd already started to ignore me as punishment for the separation to come, filled the boot of my Land Rover with kit bags, and Clare drove me to the airport. Conversation was minimal, both of us sharing unspoken anxiety about the expedition. This was Everest. We both knew of the potential difficulties that lay ahead. Three months apart is a long time and Clare would be running the house without me. 'Thank God for Elaine', I thought to myself. Steve and Lou were great too, keeping Clare occupied and giving her the love that I couldn't in my absence. We are lucky to have such great friends.

'Take good care and come back safe. Remember, the summit will always be there next year if things don't go to plan.' Clare looked deep into my eyes when she said this, and I could tell she meant it. I hugged her, told her I loved her, and then kissed her goodbye. The expedition had begun. For most of the flight to Nepal, I was going over my kit. For all expeditions, I get my equipment out in the spare room, laying most of it out on the bed. This process makes it easy for me to subtract from it or add to it as days go by. It takes me weeks to feel comfortable that I have all of the right things ready for packing. And this part of the preparation was as important as the physical and mental preparation required to embark on an expedition such as this.

I arrived at Kathmandu and was met by Dave. He was from Alpine Ascents, a well known climbing company with whom I'd decided to make the trip to Everest. Nobody had a bad word to say about Alpine Ascents and Dave had stood on the summit of Mount Everest twice before, so his credentials were sound. We instantly got on, sharing a love of running, coffee and climbing. Back at the hotel, I met the other members of our team. Vern I'd met before on Denali. He was to be our other Western guide. He was eccentric, which I liked, strumming a small guitar that he carried everywhere, and was himself a veteran of Everest ascents. I'd read about him previously, and knew he was a strong and brave climber, having successfully undertaken the first winter ascent of Denali solo. This was an incredible achievement, and commanded respect. Lapka Rita was our final guide; he was also in charge of the Sherpa. He and

Dave had been friends for many years, and he now lived with his family near Dave in Seattle. My climbing partners were again from all walks of life. Jacques was a transplant surgeon from Belgium. With some good climbs behind him, this was his first expedition to Everest. Suzanne was aiming to be the first American woman to climb the highest mountain on each continent as well as going to both poles. Kate was returning to Everest to also try and complete the 'Seven Summits'. She had been unsuccessful the previous year, but had reached a commendable 23,000 feet before turning back from camp 3 on the Lhotse face with ill health. Geri was Austrian. A retired teacher, he now climbed and cycled his way around the world. He was an insulin-dependent diabetic, and was aiming to become the first diabetic to summit Mount Everest. Chris was from Reno, in Nevada. A lawyer by trade, he showed a dry sense of humour that had me amused from the start. He had a strong climbing c.v. and had recently successfully summitted Ama Dablam, a difficult climb also in the Himalaya, which Dave had been leading. And that was it, my climbing family for the next three months of my life. We would eat, drink, sleep, walk, talk, toilet, laugh and climb together, trusting each other with our lives at the end of the same rope.

The next couple of days followed a familiar routine. We went through our kit together, talked through the itinerary, shared stories and got to know our new team mates. Before we set off there was time to explore Kathmandu, a chance to see the pyres on the banks of the river Ghanji, the burning bodies of those recently departed, set alight by loved ones. We visited some of the temples, and selected some artefacts to make base camp life more bearable. I bought a small rug to place on the floor of my tent to make it more homely, much to the amusement of the team. However, having spent many nights in tents previously, I was acutely aware of how cold the floor can get when the thin nylon is resting on frozen ice.

The itinerary was straightforward. At 29,035 feet above sea level, the highest mountain on earth would be tackled by 'siege technique', the process of laying hold to a series of camps up the mountain before attempting the summit, similar to the pattern of my previous expeditions. We would travel to Syangboche by helicopter, then trek back to Namche, where our acclimatisation would begin at 12,467 feet. After a couple of days there, we would begin the ten-day trek into Everest base camp on the south side of the mountain at 17,590 feet, travelling from the Dudh Kosi valley, up through the Imja Drangka and finally onto the Khumbu Glacier. Along the way we would visit the villages on Tengboche, Pheriche and Lobouche, all of which are fascinating in their own right, and offer spectacular views of the Himalaya and Everest. Once at base camp, we would establish a full communications tent, set up mess tents, and generally establish our team base. The climb itself up the mountain would consist of camps at 19,500 feet (camp1), at the top of the treacherous Khumbu Ice Fall. Camp 2 would be in the Western Cwm, at 21,000 feet. This would be our Advanced Base Camp (ABC). From ABC, we would establish our camp 3 at 23,500 feet on the Lhotse Face (Lhotse being another 8,000 metre giant sitting on the shoulder of Everest). Camp 4 (26,300 feet) was on the South Col, perched between Lhotse and Everest, and would be our last camp before the summit. Summit day, as always, would be long, starting at 10pm. Oxygen would be used by all, and we would travel along the South East Ridge to the South Summit. From here, we would traverse about a thousand feet to the Hillary Step, an awkward rock and ice ascent named after Sir Edmund Hillary, the first climber to successfully summit Everest, then on to the summit. We would use an absolute 'turnaround time', at which point, no matter where we had reached on the mountain, we would turn around and head back to camp 4. Being caught in 'summit fever', a compulsion to continue to try to reach the summit despite pace, conditions and time of day, could easily prove fatal, and no exceptions would be made for anyone, under any circumstances.

I looked eagerly around the room as Dave was explaining the plan. Everyone was silent, avidly paying attention to one of the two men in the room that had stood atop this great mountain, the mountain that had been the epicentre of our dreams, our thoughts and our lives for many years – in my case since I was eleven years old. Smiling, attentive faces had given way to thoughtful, questioning expressions. I could see the first glimmers of self-doubt in all of us, each wondering what lay ahead. Would we be fortunate enough to see the world from its rooftop or would it just prove to be beyond one, some or all of us. Would we all be back here together in Kathmandu as a successful team, or would any of us become an Everest statistic? Of the nineteen hundred successful summits that had taken place prior to 2006, two hundred had died in their attempts on Everest. These were the statistics that we all knew about but couldn't contemplate becoming part of, the statistics that our friends and family at home knew, but didn't speak of. 'No, it will be fine this year,' I thought to myself. The stats are saying that climbing on this great mountain is becoming safer. Most of the bodies are lying unattended in the 'Death Zone', that area above 27,000 feet where the human body can no longer acclimatise, where there is only one-third the concentration of oxygen in the air, where life is sucked rapidly from anyone who ventures into the territory and climbers can only survive for a short period of time...

By early April, we were well into the trek to base camp. Since meeting Chris Bonington, I'd always thought that if I ever did get to have a closer look at Everest, it would be from the South Side. The route from the south held a particular fascination for me. It was the side that had first given rise to the successful summit in 1953 by Sir Edmund Hillary and Tenzing Norgay. It had all the landmarks that I had so much wanted to see: the Khumbu Icefall, the Western Cwm, the Lhotse face, the Geneva Spur, the South Col, the South Summit, the Hillary Step. It had also seen the mountain's worst tragedy, when in May 1996, a total of sixteen climbers died on the mountain. The Khumbu Ice Fall holds the ominous record of being the most dangerous area on the mountain, having claimed nineteen deaths up to 2009.

On the trek to base camp, we'd visited the Tengboche Monastery. This sits atop a hill at the confluence of the Dudh Kosi and the Imja Khola rivers and offers a clear view of Everest, and is one of the most important religious centres for Sherpa culture, with thirty-five monks residing inside its walls. It is surrounded by ancient main stones, flat stones with the mantra 'Om Mane Padme Hum' inscribed on them. From the monastery, I could see prayer flags fluttering constantly in the breeze coming from the high peaks. The flags were of five colours, representing the five Buddhist elements: earth, wind, fire, water and consciousness. During our visit, we offered a ceremonial scarf to the presiding monk, who in turn blessed us for a safe summit and return. We received several blessings on our journey to base camp, none more memorable than the Lama Geisha's blessing from further down the valley. During our visit to him, we were blessed with silk scarves, given a cord necklace, which he placed around each of our necks, before presenting us with some auspicious dates for summiting the mountain. May 19th, 20th and 26th were the dates, the very sound of which had my heart thumping with excitement. These would be the days when we would most likely expect to be at the top. As a final blessing, the Lama presented us each with a card depicting the history of Mount Everest, and wrote well-wishing words inside. He told us to take a picture at the top, holding this card, and to pray for a safe descent, and send him a copy if possible.

We reached Everest base camp on April 10th 2006. Base camp was a hive of activity by the time we arrived. There were tents, teams and scientists from all over the globe, most continents represented and brightly coloured prayer flags bursting into life as the wind breathed its way up and down the valley. The smells from eager cooks rustling up meals for climbing teams, desperately wanting to impress in the hope of securing work for the following season. Nepalese workers are poorly paid in their villages, yet a climbing Sherpa can often earn up to $600 a day for his services on Everest, making working for the commercial teams on the mountain highly desirable. The dangers associated with their profession are well documented, but without their skill and input many of the teams would fail miserably. We picked our way carefully over the moraine of ice boulders, translucent pools of frozen water, yak dung and dust towards the Alpine Ascent tents at the far side of base camp, close to the start of the Khumbu Ice Fall. This was it; we were at Everest Base Camp. Next stop, the mountain itself. On our arrival, little snow lay on the ground, but we knew to expect change. Whilst the season so far had been relatively dry, we all understood that the weather could turn at any time. Once inside my tent, I set about making it homely. My rug from Kathmandu on the floor; my 'day kit' laid out neatly inside the tent, my inflated mattress on one side, and my pee-bottle placed by the side of my new bed. I took out my marker pen and retraced the word PEE on the side of the plastic bottle, desperate not to repeat the night-time confusion of drinking from the wrong bottle, as had happened twice on Denali. Had it been my own urine on both occasions, I wouldn't have been that concerned, but alas I was now all too familiar with James's pee. This would be my home for the next eight weeks or so, and any luxury item that I'd brought from home would help the days and nights pass more easily. I had a small iPod, which I rarely listened to except at night, when it provided me with some company and took my mind away from Clare and the dogs. I always missed them more in the early hours. I'd also come prepared with an inflatable pillow, so much more civilised than stuffing a fleece into a bag and using that to rest my head on at night. I'd learnt that from my previous expeditions.

All the prayer flags that I'd received on the trek in were placed behind my day-kit, my books rested by my pillow and head torches placed within easy reach of my sleeping bag. I was set. The view from my tent was straight up the Ice Fall, framed by the West Shoulder of Everest on the left, Nuptse on the right, and the Lhotse Face on its shoulders. The task ahead was a mammoth one, but I felt ready for it.

After a few restless nights' sleep, largely altitude-related, the team met to discuss the serious business of the climb. We were a small team, which meant that we could all climb together and didn't need to be split into climbing rotas. All of us appeared in good health, though Geri, delighted to have two doctors on the team, thoughtfully rotated questions and requests for examinations between Jacques and myself, eagerly applying for sympathy at his many imaginary ailments. Reassurance was the order of the day...every day. The team was gelling well, and we all looked out for each other. Suzanne was going through relationship problems at the time, and we all took turns in talking her problems through. I liked Suzanne, she was a good athlete, a great team player, and had a heart of gold. After Dave had given the team talk, we decided we would head up through the infamous Ice Fall the following day, departing at 5am. Of course, I'd be up at 3am, preparing myself thoroughly.

Before the ascent, we were involved in a Puja. Puja is the most popular form of worship practised in almost every Hindu household, both on a daily basis, and during important religious functions and ceremonies. It can be either a simple ritual, or a very complicated one. For the purpose of climbing Everest, it involves calling on deities to grant climbers and Sherpa a safe passage. We prayed together for safety, listened to chants and mantra, then said our own prayers for guidance. We had our ice axes and crampons blessed, offered food and drink at the altar of stones – and then covered each other in sampa flour. I then retired to my tent to reflect upon the day's activities and discussions, and to take some quiet time to focus on the task ahead. I'd be ready for the early departure.

The night was spent checking all the relevant climbing gear, then rechecking, then checking again. I snatched a few hours sleep and then it was time to start getting ready. It was cold that morning, and getting out of my sleeping bag was a struggle. As my body squirmed into life in the sub-zero temperatures, I had to avoid touching the sides of the tent, as tiny icicles would fall from the inside of the roof. Mornings were always the hardest, lying on the Thermarest insulating mattress, needing a pee, thirsty and hungry, yet striving to deny all of these bodily urges for just ten more minutes of warmth and rest in my cocoon.

It was 4.15am. I was out of my tent, fully dressed, in harness, climbing gear and head torch. I felt great. The moon shone down on the ice field ahead, laying a calm over the pre-dawn. I knew this was where the danger started, but our team would be OK, we had to be. We'd all trained too hard to fail, and invested too much time and money to make a return trip. As far as I was concerned, along with some of the others on the team, this was a once-in-a-lifetime attempt on the world's highest mountain. Clare, mum and dad, and my partners at work would not take kindly to me returning to this giant playground. I ate some food in the mess tent, packed some chocolate bars and raisins, and drank copious amounts of coffee. I filled my water bottles with two litres of tepid ice melt, rechecked my rucksack, and was ready to go. It was 5am, and only three other team members were ready. I started to hover around the tents nervously. Dave had said 5am, we need to leave at 5am, 'why aren't the others ready?' I muttered to myself. Eventually I calmed down, realising that fretting about others not being ready was almost as stressful as being the last man out. Everyone finally hauled themselves out of camp at 6am. We were an hour behind schedule and I was not happy. The reason for an early departure when climbing is that when it's cold, the ice is as stable as possible. Bridges made from snow over crevasses are safer, and climbing through the snow is easier. As the day warms up, melting takes place, the snow becomes sticky to walk on and through, needing more effort, and snow bridges become unstable, opening up the mouths of these giant crevasses, waiting to swallow the inattentive climber, entombing them in their depths for a decade or more, until melting lets the glacier release them at the bottom. The Ice Fall had become the last resting place of twelve climbers prior to our expedition in 2006, and we did not want to see that figure rise.

By 9am, we were mid-way up the Khumbu. The climbing was hard, across a jumbled terrain of giant ice boulders the size of houses, round even bigger seracs, up, down, and across aluminium ladders, sometimes strapped four together with ropes, laid across enormous crevasses up to three hundred feet deep in places. Great care had to be taken crossing these, keeping the guide ropes either side of the ladders taut to help provide some support, then gingerly laying a foot along the ladder, trying desperately to avoid snagging the point of the crampon. The sound of metal crampons scraping on aluminium rungs filled the morning air, along with our laboured breathing as we strained to filter some useful oxygen from what we sucked in. Great care and concentration were needed at all times in the Ice Fall; there was no room for error. I spent my time alternating between being terrified by the terrain, and entranced by the beauty of it. After all, what a privilege it was to be alive and climbing in such a place. Suddenly my trance was broken. 'CRACK', first one loud rasp through the silent air, breaking my breathing rhythm. 'BOOM' another massive ear-piercing blow. I looked ahead but all I could see was dust and ice clouding over thirty feet high further up the Ice Fall. Dave climbed fast, trying to reach the source of the noise. By the time we reached him, the news was tragic. Three climbing Sherpa had been buried underneath a giant ice block that had broken away from its cliff. We could see where their ropes disappeared into the ice; there was no movement, no sound, and no signs of struggle. The Khumbu had claimed three more victims. The scene was horrible, almost as if the three had never been there at all, just empty rope and one unattached rucksack lying on the ground. A rescue attempt was immediately mounted, but it was hopeless. The lifeless bodies lay deep down under hundreds of tons of ice, cementing them into early graves. The photographs in their tents were now ghosts of the lives that they once had. I felt sick. Suddenly it was real again; climbing can kill, and frequently does. We have little if any control over this environment. It behaves in its own unpredictable fashion, and here was the evidence. Three dead climbers – my God, they were one hour ahead of us up the Khumbu. We would have been there, exactly there, if we had left camp at 5am. My peripheral vision closed in, I felt faint. I supported myself on my axe, lowered myself to the ice, and then threw up. 'Thank God we left camp late,' I thought. This was then almost immediately replaced by a feeling of survivor guilt. I felt awful, not knowing whether relief and sadness were allowed to be compatible in such a situation, tears in my eyes for the lost climbers and the grief their families would experience at this tragic accident. We stopped our ascent at that point. The mood was solemn, the team tearful and introverted. We climbed back down to Base Camp to take stock of the situation. Suzanne came close to leaving the expedition that afternoon. She had witnessed what happens when things go wrong on Everest and was wondering whether this selfish sport was really worth the risk. Everyone retired early to their tents to think about the future of the expedition. We would have a day of mourning and respect for our lost friends the following day, perform another Puja the day after, before it would be time to venture once more into the deadly Ice Fall. Anyone wishing to depart would be helped back to Namche the following day, then on to Kathmandhu.

No-one left the team. I wrestled with the demons in my head, but concluded that we all know the risks of what we do. Admittedly, sometimes we don't want to understand or let them be properly calibrated in our heads, but fundamentally we do know the risks. A sport without challenge is not a sport, more a pastime. I'd seen death in the mountains before, when the brothers had tragically been killed on Denali, but this had been worse. These three Sherpa had been killed where we had planned to be. But we hadn't been for some reason. It hadn't been our time.

Two days later we headed into the Khumbu once more. The goal this time was to reach camp 2, ABC, at 21,000 feet, at the head of the Western Cwm, at the base of the giant Lhotse Face. Again, it was an early start, 5am, I got myself ready well in time but did no hovering to jolly along my team mates; thinking that what was meant to be was meant to be. We will leave when we are meant to leave, and not before. I was not looking forward to going back into the Ice Fall. It was a deadly place and put the fear of God into me. The team climbed swiftly and efficiently that morning, and by 11am we were nearing the top. I was sweating. It was hard work forcing the empty air into my gaping mouth, eagerly searching for any morsels of oxygen to be found in the rarefied atmosphere. My legs screamed to rest as the blood, devoid of its usual gaseous nutrition, thumped its way from their depths and back to my heart. My eyes were stinging as the cold sweat rolled down my forehead, dragging with it crusting salt and sun cream, running down the wrinkles of my squinting face and into any available gap behind my sunglasses. The mixture of sunscreen and old sweat continually pained my conjunctiva, but rubbing just made things worse. I was getting tired. 'Heads up!' came the cry from Vern, just in front of Jacques. Alerted, I looked up the hill. There was a big avalanche heading our way from the West Shoulder of Everest. Without thinking, I instinctively ducked down behind the giant ice boulder in front of me. There had been no time to plan any other escape route and I was lying on top of another climber. Someone then threw himself down on top of me. 'Rrrroar!' 'Whoooosh!' I held my breath and prayed once more. The leading edge of the avalanche came rolling towards us, and then over the top of our makeshift shield. Suddenly any air that had been present was sucked away creating a vacuum, leaving my aching, craving lungs completely empty. I tried to inhale, but choked violently instead. I held my breath again for as long as I could, and then exhaled the last remnants of breath from my body. Before I could inhale again, it was over. I breathed forcibly for two or three breaths, and then raised my head slowly from its protective wall. 'That was lucky' exclaimed Vern, 'It just missed us'. Apparently the bulk of the avalanche had just skirted the side of our path, covering instead a giant causeway thirty feet below our team, fortunately where no-one had been. 'Shit!' I thought to myself, 'If that was close, what the hell would have happened if it had hit us?' From then on, I had a huge amount of respect for the Khumbu. As far as I was concerned, I wanted to get through it as quickly as was humanly possible. I feared that someone somewhere was telling me that this was not a place that humans should be, and we went there at our peril.

After dropping off some supplies at camp 1, we climbed on to camp 2 after a brief rest. The route was easier than the climb to camp 1, consisting of wide, deep crevasses crossed by more aluminium ladders lashed together with climbing rope, and a steady incline. The path took a zigzag through the Cwm, with breathtaking views from every angle. As dusk settled in, we were finally at camp 2. We would rest here for two days; hike to the base of the revered Lhotse Face, then return down the mountain to let our bodies heal from this series of insults.

Looking up the Lhotse Face filled me with dread. The deep blue sheer ice, angled at up to 70 degrees in 2006, looked difficult at best. Parts of the ice climb had been anchored with fixed lines – ropes that we could jig up with our ascenders; the remainder would be scrambled up as best we could. There was only one fixed rope, and already I could foresee difficulty in passing slower climbers, people descending on the same rope, and relying on just one line for several people. Over the years, the Face has been the site of many accidents. On our next foray up the mountain from base camp, our target would be to make camp at the top of the Face, at 23,500 feet. Two days later, I was back in the relatively thick air of base camp. We had decided to continue our acclimatisation by repeating the journey to camp 2 two days later, then on to camp 3. We would rest one night at camp 3, without oxygen, then descend back down the valley to

8,000 feet for a few days rest, letting our bodies heal and getting fuelled up on good food before returning for our summit attempt. A fairly settled period of weather followed, allowing us to move back up the mountain. The climb up the Lhotse Face lived up to my expectations: it was nasty. Ice shavings rained down on me from the climbers' boots ahead. The rope continually iced up, causing my ascending jumar to fail to lock its teeth into the rope, resulting in a slip back down the rope a few feet. The sun was unforgiving, penetrating through my clothing causing small burns anywhere that hadn't been protected – the sides of my thighs through the venting zips in my climbing trousers, under my arms where more vents were positioned, inside my mouth and on my tongue from reflection off the crystal blue ice, the backs of my hands through my thin day-climbing gloves. It was ugly. The night at camp 3 remains one of my most unpleasant on any trip. In the rarefied atmosphere sleep was impossible, instead just restless periods of headaches, tiredness, thirst and cold. I doubted my ability to climb further up this great mountain, though I discussed this with no-one. I measured my oxygen saturations on a small meter that I'd taken with me. Normal saturation at sea level would be 100%; intensive care units at hospitals welcome patients in with saturations of 50-90%. Mine read 43%. Amazingly, I was still alive. The body can adapt to incredible changes in its environment, though I was aware that the low levels of oxygen were playing tricks on me. After spending forty minutes trying to put my left climbing boot onto my right foot, I realised that I'd have to be really cautious on the descent. Easy to make these sorts of mistakes in the safely of the tent, but if I made any whilst descending 60-70 degrees of ice, leading to a jumbled mass of crevasses 1,000 feet below, it would be more serious.

Back at base camp we packed up a few belongings for our descent down the valley. We all needed this time out, time off the hill away from the cold, the ice and our tents. We eagerly trekked down to a teahouse that we'd stopped at on the way up. The mood was jovial, we had all worked hard, made it to 23,500 feet so far, and none of us had had any real difficulties other than what one would expect at that altitude. The valley was beautiful, rhododendrons had flowered everywhere, the grass had regained its colour, and the air smelt perfumed compared to the empty vapour that sits over base camp. The teahouse provided a welcome rest. We stayed there for four days, taking hot showers, eating fine food, playing cards and chatting.

A call to Clare reassured me that all was in order at home. All members put on some weight, essential for the upcoming summit attempt, when one could easily burn 15,000 calories a day climbing and breathing rapidly up the hill. Soon our stay in relative luxury was over. The owner said a prayer for us, placed a silk scarf around each team member's neck, and we set off back to the hardships that waited for us at base camp and beyond.

At base camp, there had been some noticeable melt. The platform that my tent stood in, constructed of thick ice in early April, now presented irregular holes in its surface. There was a small stream running partially under the floor of my tent, so I set about re-arranging the platform and diverting the river elsewhere. I could cope with the cold, the isolation and the altitude, but having my tent flood in the middle of the night would have been too much. Vern called a meeting the following day for some instruction in how to operate our oxygen systems, a key feature of ascending into the death zone. The masks were cumbersome, covering the nose and mouth with sponge and canvas; they were uncomfortable and obstructed any reasonable view of our feet. They rubbed the face wherever they could, and hindered the normal pattern of inhalation and exhalation. The system worked on a free flow of oxygen into the mask, so the cylinder would remain on constantly, on 0.5 litres of flow per minute whilst sleeping, climbing with a flow of 1-1.5l/min, and occasionally turned up further for more difficult sections of the climb. We would have four to five cylinders of oxygen per person for our time battling in the death zone, and we would start to use it from camp 3 on the Lhotse Face. I worried that I would find the whole system too dolorous, but took comfort from the fact that everyone else felt the same. Suzanne had used the system before, when summiting Cho Oyu, another giant 8,000m peak in the Himalaya, so she was more accepting of the set-up, and reassured us that use of it becomes easier with time.

The next two days rotated around the communication tent, emailing our friends and family at home and gathering up our best wishes for the summit attempt. Clare sent me her love, asked me to keep safe and to come home soon; both she and the dogs were missing me. Mum and dad said the same, and my brother instructed me to break a leg. We set up another Puja on the afternoon of May 14th, and prepared for departure the following morning. Forecasts looked favourable for the next few days, and now was the time. This was what all the hard work had been for. We were at last ready to venture up the hill and into the death zone, and hopefully reach the top of the world. All those years and all those dreams now rested on five or six days of strong climbing, focus and luck.

The morning of May 15th was beautiful. We climbed up through the Khumbu Ice Fall once more, swiftly and with a deftness that had been lacking on the three previous occasions. We were all focussed and all wanted to gain a quick and direct passage through this deadly boulder field of giant popcorn rocks and ice. Throughout the climb I had to keep pinching myself, reminding myself that we were on our way to the summit of Everest. I so wanted to reach that point, that one small square foot of real estate that had been the subject of so many dreams over the years. I felt good, my footwork seemed steady, my breathing controlled, my legs felt strong and I was totally absorbed in the task. By 4pm, we had reached camp 2. This was an excellent effort from everyone and showed that we had acclimatised well. After a night's rest at camp 2, we were due to head up to camp 3. Kate had spent most of the night coughing and was now hurting in all her ribs from the constant effort of trying to expel sputum overnight. I checked her out, and found she had the beginnings of pneumonia. This would mean the end of her summit attempt. In an oxygen deprived atmosphere, this type of infection can often be life-threatening. She had been on antibiotics for a few days for a niggling cough further down the hill, but clearly things had progressed. After much soul-searching, she declared that she was heading down the hill, but would wait for us at base camp and follow our progress on the radios. This was a blow to all members of the team, we all liked Kate and all wished her success on this, her second attempt to summit Everest, but it was not to be. She descended to base camp with one of the Sherpa, leaving thirteen in the team including the three guides, Dave, Vern and Lapka, and five Sherpa. Our arrival the following day at camp 3 was a significant milestone in the climb. This was the point from which we would use oxygen. While some food was being prepared, we each sorted out our equipment and turned the flow rate on the oxygen regulator to 0.5 l/min. I couldn't believe how I felt; it was amazing. Suddenly, all the tiredness from my legs following the struggle up the Lhotse Face flowed away, replaced instead by hot, fresh oxygenated blood. My thoughts became crystal clear, my appetite swelled and my body felt alive. 'Wow!' I thought to myself, 'and that's just on 0.5 l/min!' I re-measured my saturation levels: 92 %, fantastic, that was way better than the previous reading at camp 3, no wonder I felt rejuvenated. We all ate and drank well that night, our first on the magic oxygen.

May 18th, 7am and we were getting ready to traverse from camp 3 to camp 4, at 26,300 feet. This was a big day for me mentally and physically. I'd been to 22,830 feet before, on Aconcagua, but this was a huge step up in altitude, and it didn't start well. Whilst getting our ropes prepared, I heard muffled shouting from above, then 'THUD!' A lifeless body lay still, just ahead of us. We rushed over, but in vain. The contorted bloodied corpse lay freezing to its resting place, feet and boots outstretched, arms broken and folded, left one behind his bent neck, right one under the torso. His poor face wore a contorted expression of pain and overwhelming fear. He had known what was unfolding before him. We tried to move him, but it was difficult. I'd once helped the ambulance team at my local hospital bring in a motorcyclist to the mortuary, recently deceased following a head-on collision with a car. As I placed my arms under the leather-clad figure, the contents of the suit was like jelly in my grasping hands. Not a single bone intact under the clothing, no rigidity or firmness to the skeleton from any position or any angle. This climber felt the same. He was a member of the Chilean team climbing ahead. His team members were visible in the distance high up on the mountain. He had not been clipped to any safety line and had paid the ultimate price. We did what we could, which under the circumstances was very little, other than place him in a more dignified position as his team members descended the rope to attend to the situation.

Slowly but purposefully we moved towards the Geneva Spur. I was behind the Austrian, Geri, who was coughing regularly and swearing to himself in his native tongue. This part of the climb was a huge challenge for him; his diabetes required the utmost care at this height so there was no room for error or misjudgement with his blood sugars. Suzanne was strong, climbing confidently up ahead with Chris. I preferred to lead from the back, enjoying some discussions with Jacques on our differing roles in medicine. We reached camp 4 in good time, settling into our tents by 4pm. Camp 4 was a truly desolate place, clearly a place that humans were not welcome, or likely to survive in for long. Occasional discarded oxygen cylinders and ripped remnants of tents from teams in previous years coloured the otherwise barren landscape. There was little snow this high, the 200mph-plus winds ravaging any drifts from the Col, both pre-

and post-monsoon. The summit window on Everest relies on warm air moving across the Bay of Bengal, travelling up the Himalaya and pushing the jet stream northwards. This potentially drops the winds at the top from 200mph to 10-30mph, enabling summits if everything else is in the climber's favour.

We fed and watered ourselves as best we could, some of us choosing granola bars over noodle soup and porridge. I'd been lucky at the higher altitudes; my appetite had remained strong, and I had been 'fuelling my furnace' at every opportunity. Initially we had planned to rest the night of the 18th May, but Dave had come round to our tents asking us all individually how we felt. The forecast for the next few days didn't look so good now. We had access to two independent forecasting systems, one from America and one from Switzerland. They differed slightly from each other, but the general trend was one of worsening weather high up. The traverse over the Geneva Spur and across the Yellow Band had been relatively straight-forward in climbing terms, and Dave was considering mounting a summit attempt that night. None of us declined the opportunity of going up a day early. 'The sooner we summit, the sooner we get down from this hellhole' I thought to myself. I'd not seen Clare, had a bath, or a decent nights' sleep in two months and I was as keen as the rest to press on, but the decision turned against us. We left camp 4 at 10pm, to light winds and some swirling snowfall. Already ahead I could see a short line of bobbing head torches snaking up the Triangular Face, the first obstacle in the path from camp 4 to the summit. It was a cold night, the moon barely visible through the cloud which was depositing its snow at the Col. I'd checked, double-checked and triple-checked all the fastenings of my equipment, my crampons, rucksack and oxygen supply, and all had seemed in order. As soon as we left the high camp, the snow bursts thickened, reducing visibility to a few feet. The winds continued to pick up, and by midnight things were bad. The snow was heavy, the winds now strong, throwing ice and powder into every corner of my clothing. I couldn't see the climber in front or the climber behind, not even their head torches. Visibility was virtually nil, and this was dangerous. Aware that a few feet either side of the path that we were creating up the face, there lay a 6,000 foot drop on either side, waiting to claim any unsuspecting climber blinded and lost in the conditions.

My mind raced back to 1996, scene of the worst disaster to strike climbers on the mountain, when ten people lost their lives to a storm. Some had wandered off the path, fallen and died; others had simply frozen where they sat. This could replicate 1996, and I felt real fear for the first time on Everest. I decided that it was time to turn around and retrace my steps if I could, back to high camp. These conditions were not compatible with success, safety or indeed life, and some would lose theirs if we continued. Just at that moment, from the blackness that engulfed me, I felt a prod on my right shoulder. I turned quickly, alarmed to feel something when I had been so alone, breaking my steps as I'd climbed to the sound of my deep and quickening breaths. 'We're gonna turn around' shouted a voice, the mouth positioned right at my ear, hollering to be heard above the ferocious howl of the wind. It was Dave, his voice unmistakable. I kept close to his boots, visible now by my head torch, no more than a foot away from me. I was not going to let him out of my sight. Camp 4 seemed like an oasis to me now, and I was desperate to get back there safely and in the presence of company. As we climbed down towards camp, I was amazed to see another team continuing to head up. Adventure Consultants, a commercial climbing outfit from New Zealand, also had a team on Everest that year. 'Brave... or stupid?' I thought to myself, as they quickly disappeared into the black storm.

Back at high camp we rested and took stock of the situation. We'd all been beaten up a little in the storm, and were happy to get back to the relative haven of the tents. I'd noticed Geri wasn't drinking much, and remarked on this, suggesting he try and force some more fluid in. He wasn't taking much notice, instead choosing to get into his sleeping bag for some rest. As dawn came, the winds showed no signs of abating. We rehydrated, ate food, and watched intently for a sign that things would improve. Amazingly, the Adventure Consultants team had summited in the small hours of the morning, though not all team members had got to the top. However, they were all now safely back at camp 4. I couldn't help but feel a bit envious of those that had reached the top and returned safely – that was, until I spoke with them. Conditions had been so poor that they'd hardly seen anything from the summit, arriving in darkness and heading back down to the relative safety of 26,300 feet. The round trip from high camp to the top and back had been sixteen hours for them, and if we got another chance it would be about the same.

All day on the 19th May we looked out of our tents waiting for the wind to abate, but it didn't look like it was going to oblige. We continued eating and drinking, most of us, and praying for a break in the conditions. The two forecasts on the radio were different, the American one suggesting no change, the Swiss one predicting decent weather up top, but the fact remained that with high winds at camp 4, the only way was down. We decided we would rest out the day, then head down on the 20th if conditions warranted. I remembered the card given to me by the Lama Geisha in the monastery, and the instructions that we'd been given to take a picture holding it at the summit. I pulled it from my rucksack and held it to the mountain, pointing towards the triangular face, and quietly prayed for a change in the weather. To my complete surprise, the wind simultaneously dropped. The tent sides no longer needed a body draped at each corner to prevent it from buckling and infolding. I eagerly tucked the card back in my sack. 'Now that is weird,' I thought to myself. 'Maybe the Swiss forecast is correct,' muttered Dave. He then got on the satellite phone to discuss the weather with the American forecaster. Dave, Chris and I were in one tent, Jacques, Suzanne, Geri and Vern in another. During Dave's conversation with the forecast service, it was obvious that they too now expected calm conditions at the summit. My heart was pounding, my mouth getting dry as Dave broke the news to the team. 'Things look settled now for twenty-four hours or so, we'll try for the summit tonight.' This was great news. Two team members were not keen on continuing, but after several rounds of discussions, everyone was on board for the summit attempt. We would leave at 9pm.

Time passed quickly that afternoon, all of us wrapped in our own thoughts about the evening to come. Geri again asked me to check him over, which I duly did, remarking on the fact that he was a little dehydrated and should have more fluid. He knew the key to success was looking after himself. I chatted with Dave and Chris about the route above where we had turned around the previous night, ate plenty and checked my oxygen equipment once more. As darkness fell again in the Death Zone, the bobbing of head torches behind canvas signified that climbers were once more readying themselves for battle. The crisp, silence of the night was intermittently broken by the sounds of climbers coughing and groaning, as once more their exhausted bodies were asked to perform. Down suits were zipped up, crampons could be heard clanking on loose rock around the tents, and stoves were being fired up once more to replenish empty water bottles before departure. Another dolorous night lay ahead but, hopefully, this time it would have a better outcome. By 8pm, we were all up and ready. It was dark but the sky was clear. The atmosphere was different from the previous night, we were all guarded with our expectations, now acutely aware that no matter how well the training had gone at home, how well the acclimatisation had gone on the mountain, or how good the equipment that we were using, ultimately mother nature held the trump card.

We left at 10pm precisely. This pleased me, and settled me into a strong rhythm. I found climbing on the oxygen really good. My hands and feet were warm, my brain working accurately. My flow rate was set at 1l/min, and that was plenty. Soon we were passing the position of the previous day's retreat, and heading towards the Balcony. Our 'turn-around' time for the day was twelve noon: if we were not descending by that time, we had all agreed that we would go back, no matter where we were on the hill. Being in the Death Zone is one thing, but being stuck in it without cover, oxygen and fluids after dark is another. My breathing rate had settled to thirty breaths a minute – this is over double the sea-level rate but it was comfortable at this altitude. With every two breaths I stepped forward, shuffling a path up the triangular face and toward the Balcony. The night air was lifeless, our bodies robotic as we proceeded forwards and upwards. Step, breathe, rest, breathe, then step again – that was my routine. Nothing but the sound of ice speared by sharp crampon points and the rustle of down suit on canvas rucksack strap, minute after minute, hour after hour, into the frozen night. I had to temper my pace: too quick and the sweat rolled down my fatigued body, then froze against my skin as the bitter air met it further down my torso, too slow and the muscles seized, the fingers cramped around my ice axe, and my thought processes slowed. This mountain was brutal, but nobody ever said it would be easy. This was no time to be reckless; we were in the Death Zone, climbing the highest mountain in the world.

We reached the Balcony in good time after three hours or so, and used that as a landmark to switch to full oxygen cylinders and leave our half-used cylinders there for the descent. At the cylinder change, Dave started chuntering to himself. 'What's up big man?' I shouted over. 'Bloody cylinder is empty!' came the reply. The spare oxygen cylinder that Dave had carried up in his rucksack was an empty one. I laughed. At camp 4, I had

had a conversation with Dave, and he'd carefully instructed me on how to tell a full oxygen cylinder from an empty one. 'It's easy', he'd said, 'you can tell by the feel and the weight.' And so it was, but Dave had carried 3kg of useless metal a thousand feet up Everest. We both roared, he'd seen the funny side of it. We had some spare cylinders so hopefully this wasn't, going to present a problem. It was 1am, the skies were still clear, and the whole team seemed to be going well. I was running my oxygen system on very low flow, 0.5 l/min. I didn't seem to need more, and this rate fed my body well. It also provided a comforting safety net for me in the event of any problems. It would allow extra usage at higher flow rates later if I ran into any problems, and this made me feel 'safe', if one could possibly experience such emotion at almost five vertical miles up from sea level. The ground underfoot from the balcony was firm, ice and rock bands mainly, making climbing tricky in places. Crampons are perfect for ice, but a hindrance on rock, the points scratching their way down the stone like fingernails down a blackboard. Great care was needed over these sections of rock. There is no fixed path on Everest. I'd placed myself right behind Dave, as I figured he'd have a good idea of the way, having summited twice before. 'Hey Dave', I shouted, at one of the more tricky sections, 'slow down a bit so I can follow your foot-holds.' 'There aren't any', came the reply, 'just find what you can.' And so I did, scrambling, climbing and slipping my way upward, crampons twisting and scraping. Time passed quickly. It was 4am when I next looked at my watch, and there was no wind. Conditions were perfect, all we needed now was sunrise, and to feel the warmth that it would bring to our faces, and the light that it would bring to our route. My head torch was dimming, and the circumference of light that it threw on the rough terrain in front was decreasing. I looked to my right, and could just see a faint orange line spreading from right to left on the horizon. Dawn was not far away, and with it would come relief. Ahead of me, Dave was sitting down, taking his boots off. 'You OK mate?', I exclaimed, wondering why Dave would be removing his boots at minus 30. 'No, bloody feet are freezing!', he shouted. I sat down beside him, he took his boots off, and I unzipped my down suit. 'Put your feet in here', I shouted, pointing to my unzipped chest. Dave put his feet next to my thermal top, and I pulled the warm down around his cold toes. Twenty minutes later his feet had settled, responding to the warmth of my body. He retied his boots and we set off once more into the darkness. 'This next part is tricky,' Dave said. 'Take care, the ridge is only a foot wide.' I'd read of this traverse, and knew that on either side of this thin ridge lay a 6,000 feet drop to Nepal on one side, and Tibet on the other. There was absolutely no room for error here. Chwang, the climbing Sherpa who had been assigned to climb with me, was superb. He climbed right behind me the entire route, ensuring my path stayed true. Again on the traverse, he guided me along the path. The traverse didn't concern me as much as I thought it would, mainly because I could not see the drop on either side. By 5am, we had reached the South Summit of Everest, and dawn was breaking. From the South Summit I could now see multiple peaks along the line of the Himalaya, each over 20,000 feet, yet dwarfed by the giant that we were on. I took another picture, both of the view and of myself, broke another six-inch clump of solid ice from the exhaust valve of my face mask, and looked ahead. I didn't dare let myself even dream that reaching the summit was within my grasp. An hour later, and we were at the Hillary Step, a 50-foot rock, snow and ice outcrop in the route, that needs to be tackled successfully to proceed. At sea level, this would be easy, but at 28,500 feet, in temperatures of minus 30, in full climbing regalia, with the intrusion of an oxygen mask obscuring vision, it's not. Once again Chwang was there, showing me the best line to take, and helping me select a good rope from the endless tatters of ropes that lay before me from previous expeditions dating back decades. Huffing, heaving and pulling, I eventually got to the top of the Hillary step. The path ahead looked straightforward. I could see colour moving in the distance, and squinting into the dawn sun I could make out its origin. There were prayer flags, placed on the summit. Half an hour later and the end was within our grasp, my pace had quickened, my breathing relaxed, my ice axe planted firmly with every footstep. Nothing around me worried me any more, this was it, and I was going to summit. Tears started rolling down both cheeks, I had to raise my goggles to refocus my vision. My mind went back to 1975 and my meeting with Sir Chris Bonington, and my thoughts then of how I'd dreamt of what the world would look like from its highest point, what smell it would have, and what the air would feel like against my skin.

At 7.02am on the 20th May 2006 I had my own answers to these questions. There was nothing in front of me. At that moment Sir Chris Bonington and I shared one thing in common, one footprint, and that was enough. I stood on the top, raised my arms aloft, and gazed at the unimaginable beauty that lay before my eyes. No amount of superlatives could ever describe what my fortunate eyes devoured at that moment, hungry for more of every view, to gather lifelong memories. I took my oxygen mask off, preferring instead to breathe in the rarefied air that engulfs these peaks. The air tasted clear, totally clear, unpolluted by anything. The mountains below looked up at us. To my left, I could see far down the Rhongbuk Glacier and into Tibet, and on my right the path that we had trodden upwards to the summit. In the full dawn it looked spectacular, ridges, seracs, rock faces, gullies, strewn boulders and giant overhangs of snow and ice, balanced at almost impossible angles, defying gravity until nudged by a few more snowflakes. Dead ahead lay the glorious silhouette of Makalu, another giant of the Himalaya, and in the distance, far far in the distance, the outline of Kanchenjunga. Everything had worked out. The weather had co-operated, the team had climbed well, and everyone in our team had reached the summit. Chris and I hugged on the top, took pictures of each other and the views, and then said a small prayer for Bongo, Chris's dog that had lost its battle for survival against age while he'd been away. I sat down next to Dave, hugged him, and thanked him for his efforts; he was a great guide, the best I'd had on any mountain.

Over an hour later, and our thoughts turned to the descent. I so didn't want to leave that tiny patch of ice elevated in space. I'd worked so hard to get there and I just didn't want to leave. 'Summiting is optional, getting down is mandatory,' I thought to myself eventually, repeating the words of Pete Athens, a world famous mountaineer. I reminded myself to take great care on the descent, as we started down. Back at the Hillary Step, I took a final look over my right shoulder at the summit. I had stood upon it. 'Wonder if I'll ever stand on it again?' I asked myself softly. Back at the South Summit we met our second group; Suzanne, Jacques and Geri. Vern and Lapka had been guiding them, along with their Sherpa companions. They were on their way up, climbing a little more slowly than us. Vern was coughing badly, and thought he had a recurrence of a pneumonia that he'd suffered a few months previously. He decided to descend from the South Summit, a sensible but difficult decision. There was no point in going up higher if his lungs were telling him not to. Geri was struggling; he looked dehydrated and appeared a little confused. 'You drinking and eating Geri?' I shouted after him, as the second group left the South Summit and headed towards the Hillary Step. I worried for Geri, his diabetes could easily get out of control up here, and if it did, it could have disastrous consequences. As I descended, it became increasingly disturbing for me to see the bodies of climbers that had lost their lives on the hill. Scattered at intervals were the multicoloured dead, mummified in the desiccating air, some lying where they had fallen, others sitting as if resting for a break then not having the energy to regain their feet. The scenes were distressing and the starkest possible reminder of the dangers of climbing in such hostile environments. Retracing my steps over the traverse was enlightening. The narrow bridge that spanned the huge drop-offs from either side sent the blood rushing to my head. I was glad I hadn't been able to see the view on the way up. I crossed the 200-foot traverse, focussing on nothing but the other side, yet at the same time being completely aware of the gulf of air that surrounded me on this exposed section. By mid-day on the 20th of May, our team was trundling back into camp 4 victorious. One of the Sherpa had prepared noodle soup for us on our return, which we devoured like hungry dogs. Two litres of fluid was all we could carry up the mountain to the summit; for fourteen hours of hard climbing, that left us probably 2-3 litres depleted in our craving bodies. Rehydration and nourishment was critical, and I had no problem rising to the challenge. The utilisation of a likely 15,000 calories or more on the summit climb had left my body exhausted and my muscles cramping from salt loss. I got on the satellite phone and called Clare. She'd been following the reports on the Internet and knew that we had reached the summit. It was an emotional phone call, she knew what this meant to me, and was obviously glad that I was safe. I phoned mum and dad too, and they were delighted.

Slowly the other half of our team made it back to high camp, first Jacques, then Suzanne, and at 4pm Geri arrived. Geri was staggering, disorientated and proving a handful for the ever-tolerant Sherpa that he was with. Another Sherpa had dropped back to assist, and Lapka was shouting at him furiously. At camp, Geri remained agitated. I checked on his insulin with Jacques; it had frozen. Geri hadn't protected his lifeline very well, choosing to ignore the constant reminders to look after himself on the mountain. He was now suffering the consequences and had put the team in a precarious position. Throughout the remainder of the afternoon and into the evening, we did what we could to control him, trying to force fluid and nutrition into him, but it was difficult. He was thrashing around; unaware that we were trying to help him, fighting everyone off insisting that he just wanted to sleep. This was a bad situation; a diabetic at 26,000 feet with no insulin, his body stressed beyond any normal tolerance, refusing to eat or drink. He had become the first diabetic to summit Everest, but nearly paid the ultimate price. We were still in the death zone, where exposed flesh can freeze irreparably in an instant, and lungs and brain swell with little notice. It was a long night. We all knew that descent the next day was essential, and that Geri's survival depended on him co-operating. We were all exhausted, and patience ran low in the small hours. I retreated to my tent, and pitied Jacques and Vern as they continued to try to get Geri to eat and drink. There was little more that I could offer, but I remained on hand just in case. He was constantly taking his oxygen mask off, not understanding that he needed it there and that without it he would surely die. Dawn broke at 6am, and with it we broke camp. The whole team was keen to move down the mountain swiftly, and then we would stay the night at camp 2. Geri proved a real handful that day. Still without insulin and not eating or drinking much, his blood sugars must have been all over the place. Dave and Vern attached him to a short rope between the two of them, and slowly wrestled him down from high camp. It was a brilliant effort from the two guides. Without their expertise, I have no doubt that Geri would have died. Lapka took over when either guide tired, and eventually we all reached the relative safety of camp 2. Coming down the perilous Lhotse Face, short-roped, Geri had taken multiple falls, only to be lifted back to his feet by one of the guides, and lowered down a bit further. It had been a nightmare for them, the worst kind. Back at camp 2 Geri recovered, the thicker air assisting greatly. He had some insulin at the camp, which hadn't frozen, and soon he regained a level of normal behaviour. It had been a close call. He'll never know quite how close, but he was very lucky to have made it down alive.

After a restful night at camp 2, we returned to base camp. On the way through the Ice Fall, I knew I was tired. I slipped into three crevasses on the way down, none of them serious fortunately, and each one easy to pull myself up from. It was only as I trudged from the bottom of the Khumbu toward the Alpine Ascent's camp that it really dawned on me. I had climbed Everest. My smile beamed from ear to ear, a small part of me still refusing to believe what had happened. And now, back at base camp, we were safe, we'd made it. I knew that this experience would give me an inner power and strength for the rest of my life. Such a huge test against Mother Nature, and we had all found, confronted and conquered our fears.

Back at base camp, we heard the terrible news about David Sharp, a climber from near my home in North Yorkshire. He was climbing alone on the north side of the mountain, and had died whilst we had been high up on the mountain. Clare had received a harrowing phone call that morning, asking her if she had been aware that a north-east man had died on Everest the previous night. She hadn't heard from me since our return to camp 4, and had naturally feared that it was me. For several long hours she waited for news. Oblivious to this, I had been descending from camp 2. When I phoned her from base camp, her relief was audible, and my anger at the reporter who'd phoned her in the early hours was intense. David had been on the other side of the mountain, and we'd heard nothing, neither had anyone high up on the South Side of Everest, but as the story broke it became one of the most controversial in the history of climbing. Reports came flooding in of David being 'left for dead' high up in the death zone on the north side, and of climbers hiking past him whilst he was still alive. The news came largely from people who had no idea what was happening, and were not best placed to report on these events. Climbing the mountain solo, without any Sherpa assistance or technology, as David had attempted to do, should be supported. However, things do go wrong, and what happened to David happens every season on Everest. David was an accomplished climber, having already summited the world's sixth highest peak, Cho Oyu, in good style. He was capable of summiting Everest. He had really hoped to climb the mountain without bottled oxygen, which is extremely dangerous. Many expeditions insist on climbers using oxygen, and on a pairing system so that no climber climbs alone. A picture had been taken of a lone climber, heading up towards the summit, late in the afternoon on May 14th; it is likely that this was David Sharp. It's probable that David had summited late, and had to descend in the dark, which is dangerous and difficult. His headlight batteries may have run down, and he found a cave and sensibly crawled in. Unfortunately, it was the coldest night of the season. Moving past David, in his state of near-death, must have been very uncomfortable, probably the worst thing that those teams had seen in their lives. The desire to reach out to someone in such need would have been enormous; to give dignity to death as the last right that any person should expect. The guides moved the team on. They had seen these things before, and recognised the inevitable outcome. It was likely that many members from various teams would give differing accounts of events that day. Hypoxia (lack of oxygen) can also play with the mind, and recollections of events are not necessarily accurate. Some of the Sherpa moved David out and into the sun, put oxygen on him, and there was some response. It took two strong Sherpa twenty-five minutes to move David four steps, and then they had to put him down again. They decided that there was no way to rescue him. Briefly, David spoke, and in his dying words, he told a Sherpa his name was David Sharp, and he was with Asian Trekking. There has been much controversy around David's death and criticism of various climbers and guides purported to have left him for dead; you only have to google his name to discover that. The leaders on David's expedition didn't know of his dreadful position until he was dead, and that is tragic. Did David expect to be rescued? It is unlikely. According to his friends and climbing companions, he would not have wanted anyone to risk their lives for him. The controversy will remain, but all climbers are aware of the risks involved; it forms part of the attraction of these expeditions to remote and hostile places.

The journey from base camp to Kathmandu was a sobering one. I stopped this time to pay special homage to the Chortons, small stone monuments built by loved ones on the hills in memory of those that have lost their lives on Everest. There were hundreds of them, everywhere. For some reason they had felt less pertinent on the walk in to base camp, but now, as I retraced my steps, I was lost in thoughts for those who had died there that year. It seemed unnerving to think that several more Chortons would be there next year, in remembrance of those who died this season.

On the plane home, I couldn't sleep. I was desperate to see Clare again, we'd been apart nearly three months and I was now really missing her. In the arrivals lounge at Newcastle airport, it was an emotional reunion, more so than my previous returns. Clare couldn't wait to update me on all the gossip from home, and I couldn't wait to test out the king-size bed again; after all, twelve weeks is a long time. Routine soon returned, erasing out the chaotic sleep and exercise pattern of Everest. Clare enjoyed having the male company back, my body athletic, muscles taut from the repetitive exercise they'd endured on the mountain. We often talked about having children, even thought of some names, but ultimately decided it would have to wait. I had my sights set on the 'Seven Summits' now, scaling the highest mountain on each of the seven continents. I had successfully climbed four, and so I soon had my books out again looking for the next adventure. The dogs enjoyed having me back too, waking me up each morning at 6am with feverish licks to my face and chest, insisting I get up, feed them and take them for a run. We generally ran for five miles each morning along the old railway track that goes from Whitby to Robin Hood's Bay, then put in a longer run of fifteen miles at the weekend through the country villages to an old Roman road. After each run, the dogs would always look at us longingly as if to say 'ok, we've rested for a good ten minutes now, can we go again?' – but that's border collies for you.

CLARE

The three months Ali was away just flew by. I was maid of honour for two friends during this time, my best friend and flatmate from university, Kirsten, and my young House-Officer, Rhiannon. On the day Ali went for the summit, I had a house full of seven girls I had never met before, an impromptu 'hen weekend' for Rhiannon. She was a medical officer in the army and had just returned from Iraq, so I did not have much time to organise her party and thought the easiest idea would be to hold it in Whitby, which is a beautiful place and an up and coming tourist destination. There were only two occasions in all of Ali's travels that I was ever extremely concerned for his safety. The first was after his initial ascent of the summit was abandoned. He called me from camp 4 and told me that some of the team were going down, but that he, Chris and Dave were going to give it another go. From my reading of other climbing disaster books, one theme common to all tragedies is that the 'team' starts to disintegrate and climbers seem to make irrational decisions, inhibited by the effects of hypoxia on the brain. I asked Ali to reconsider his decision and reminded him that Everest would still be there next year, but he was firm in his intention to continue. I was extremely anxious, but had to try and focus on my guests and ensure that Rhiannon had a good time as she had had some terrible experiences in Iraq and deserved a bit of fun. It was a helpful distraction.

On the night of the summit, Alpine Ascents were updating their web page regularly with information on the climbers' progress and I checked this every hour. I was delighted when the report came through that Ali had reached the top of the world. I was so proud of him, as I knew how many sacrifices he had made to achieve this dream. I did not get to sleep, however, until he phoned me from camp 4 and told me he was safely tucked up in his sleeping bag! The descent is often as treacherous as the ascent, as fatigue sets in and the elation of the summit clouds the climbers' judgement. Ali knew this and we had often spoken about the fact that summiting was optional but descent was mandatory! My sister Kate and Toni helped me organise a welcome home party a few days after Ali returned. He had been fortunate to reach the peak on a perfect day and the photographs and video from the summit were incredible.

Picture 1. Lazarus, my pet chicken, in my arms – both of us aged 7 years old.

Picture 2. Sir Chris Bonington (courtesy of Sir Chris Bonington).

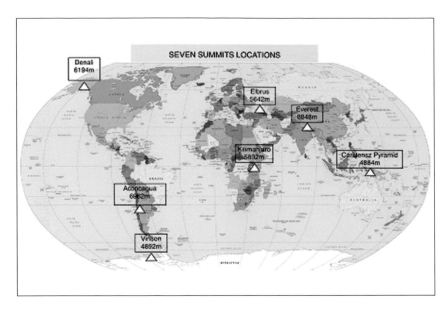

Picture 3. Location of the Seven Summits.

Picture 4. Aconcagua Summit.

Picture 5. Summit Approach Mount Vinson.

Picture 6. Summit Mount Vinson.

Picture 7. Staring at Denali.

Picture 8. Summit of Denali.

Picture 9. Early dawn, descending Denali.

Picture 10. Team at Pheriche, Mount Everest in background.

Picture 11. Lama Geisha.

Picture 12. My tent, looking up the Khumbu Ice Fall.

Picture 13. Walking through The Western Cwm, Mount Everest.

Picture 14. Sunrise by Everest South Summit.

Picture 15. South Summit Climb.

Picture 16. Standing on Mount Everest Summit.

Picture 17. The Whitby Gazette – On top of Everest.

Picture 18. Sitting, elated, on top of the world – Mount Everest Summit.

Picture 19. Summit View Mount Everest.

Picture 20. View down North Route Mount Everest.

Picture 21. Sunrise over Kilimanjaro from the summit.

Picture 22. Summit, Mount Kilimanjaro.

Picture 23. The Barrels, Mount Elbrus.

Picture 24. Elbrus Summit.

Picture 25. The Tyrolean Traverse on Carstensz Pyramid.

Picture 26. Carstensz Pyramid Summit.

Picture 27. Camels blocking the route.

Picture 28. The final route from Douentza to Timbuktu.

Picture 29. Arrival in Timbuktu.

Picture 30. Clare and I at the finish of the Chicago Marathon.

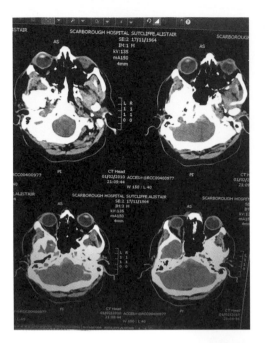

Picture 31. CAT scan of my head. Picture shows my eyes, nose, base of the brain, with blood surrounding the structures from the haemorrhage.

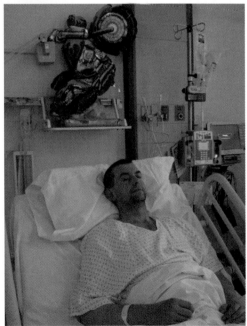

Picture 32. Hospital and my hardest climb.

Chapter 6
Kilimanjaro

It was good to get back to work. I'd missed some of the routine, and certainly wanted to catch up with my patients and see how they were all doing. General Practice was interspersed with television and radio interviews and doing articles for various newspapers, none of which I minded. From the start of climbing the Seven Summits, I'd committed myself to raising as much money as possible for St Catherine's Hospice, the local terminal care hospice in Scarborough. I'd had several patients pass through its doors, and thought the service that they provided was second to none. Funding had been difficult for them over the years, and they were grateful for any support. After Everest, and including the various marathons that I had run, the funds totalled about £25,000, mainly due to the generosity of the local community, friends and family, and I was pleased with that. I was also involved in giving climbing/motivational talks to various groups around the area, which raised further funds for the hospice, the final slide being a picture of me crouching on the summit of Everest holding the St. Catherine's Hospice flag.

I had arranged to go to Carstensz Pyramid in Western Papua in the November of 2006. Located in the Western Central Highlands, it is the highest mountain on the Oceanic continent, and is a moderate rock climb. It is notoriously difficult to get to, with political unrest obstructing most movement through the country. It's only been summited by a fraction of those that have reached the top of Everest, and I was really keen to get on the expedition. Unfortunately, having organised the necessary time away from the practice, the trip was cancelled at the last minute, largely due to increasing hostilities in the area. I spoke to the various climbing companies to see if they had any other expeditions running, but little was happening at that time of the year. Eventually I got in touch with a friend of mine, Steve, and we arranged to go to Kilimanjaro. This hastily made plan suited me well, as Kilimanjaro is another one of the Seven Summits, being the highest mountain in Africa at 19,340 feet. Most advice suggests not climbing it in the rainy season, which is November to May, but we thought we'd go and give it a try. Time was fairly limited for both Steve and I; eight days home to home would be our maximum.

Crowned by eternal snows, Kilimanjaro is the highest freestanding mountain in the world and totally dominates its landscape. Located in Tanzania, this extinct volcano incorporates five eco-systems and contains dramatic terrain. The climb is largely non-technical but would require the usual obsessive training to give the greatest chance of success.

Clare was more relaxed about this climb, we'd both known of other people who'd climbed Kilimanjaro and returned safely, and the trip was much shorter than the previous climb. The dogs were also getting used to the sight of my kit bags getting loaded up again, and didn't pay that much attention any more.

The plane landed at Kilimanjaro International Airport on November 16th 2006. I stood patiently in line, waiting to pass through passport control, but was constantly distracted by a 'click' 'click' 'click' sound, and couldn't determine where it was coming from. Eventually, I looked up at the ceiling, which was completely covered in cockroaches. The 'clicking' sound had been these, falling from the ceiling and onto my wide-brimmed hat. I removed my hat, tipped off the twenty or so roaches that were enjoying the comfort of the cotton rim, tip-toed through the multiple giant insects that decorated the floor, and passed through control. Tanzania, like most of Africa, presents a contrasting picture of extreme poverty and wealth. The journey by four-wheel drive to the hotel took us through both these extremes, though poverty was the dominant feature. Steve had organised a hotel in Moshi, which was plain but functional. We worked out an itinerary, which consisted of a fairly rapid acclimatisation climb up Mount Meru (14,947 feet), then on to Kilimanjaro. We were going to climb via a combination of the Umbwe Route and Western Breach, creating an interesting and challenging ascent away from the busier routes on the mountain, though at this time of year we were unlikely to meet up with any other groups.

After a fitful night's rest, swatting mosquitoes and flicking various unrecognisable insects from my bed sheet, we breakfasted then headed off to Meru. The climb took us just three days, as we were both under some time pressures, but prepared us reasonably well, we thought, for Kilimanjaro. It consisted of mainly rock scrambling, finally climbing the remaining part of the crater wall that surrounds the ash cone in the centre of the volcano. From the summit we had amazing views of Kilimanjaro to the east, and the plains below us. Day four of the trip saw us at the start of the Umbwe Route, which we reached by jeep. From a dusty beginning, the track wound upwards, narrowing to become barely discernible, winding up through dense jungle. The magnificent rainforest, now saturated with rain, provided us with cover for the first night at 9,840 feet. It was not a settled night. At about 3am I awoke to a scratching outside my tent. I sat up and listened for a few minutes, trying to work out what the noise was, and whether whatever was responsible for it would present any danger to me. Foolishly, I put on my head torch, and tentatively unzipped my tent to investigate. I was greeted by an equally startled Colobus monkey looking for food. I, hoping that it's gaping mouth and snarling teeth didn't indicate that I was suitable nutrition, screamed loudly at the startled monkey, then retreated with haste to the very rear of my tent to find my climbing knife. We parted company at that point, though the rest of my night was spent sitting up on guard at the back of the tent, knife blade open and firmly in the locked position! By the end of day five, we had reached the Baranco Hut, via a steep narrow ridge with a deep valley on either side. African walnut trees draped in 'goats beard' moss pointed the way. The huge ravine of the Baranco dropped away on one side. Directly ahead of it was the distinctive Breach Wall of Kilimanjaro. Once above 10,000 feet, the entire landscape changed to high moorland. The Baranco Hut, a tin shack, was our resting place that night, at 12,790 feet. The following day we climbed up the ridge to the final slopes of the volcano, affording us views of the route to the summit up the Western Breach directly above us. We camped at 15,740 feet by the Arrow Hut, and prepared for our summit day, when we would leave at 4am.

Summit day started with a climb up steep scree, illuminated by our head torches. This type of terrain is always draining – it's like walking uphill in sand. Each firmly planted foot slides backwards at the same time as the new leading foot reaches forward to gain position. Hour upon hour this monotonous repetition continued, draining my thighs and calves of all utilisable glucose and oxygen. It was colder than I had anticipated, and my feet were numb in my 3-season boots and two pairs of socks. I stopped intermittently to swing my legs, trying to bring warm blood to my toes. I wasn't keen on the fresh provisions that Steve happily ate on the climb, preferring instead to consume pre-packed and sealed snacks, the origin of which I could be a little more certain. Eventually, the scree led up past the Arrow Glacier and onto to the crater rim. Scrambling over the top of the frozen lava formations, I was relieved to see the warming, orange glow that announced the impending arrival of dawn, and the comfort that the sun would bring to my cold feet. As the sun slowly rose, I could see the giant shadow of Kilimanjaro stretching across the plains behind me towards Mount Meru. The view was mesmerising. Once at the crater we crossed the tiny Furtwangler Glacier and then made the final steep climb up to Uhuru Summit at 19,340 feet. At the summit, Steve and I hugged each other and sat down to eat some food and drink some water. It had been an exhausting schedule, but we had kept to it and had been reasonably lucky with the weather. The views from the summit were spectacular. To the north was Mount Kenya, the continent's second highest peak. Mount Meru stood to the west, with the plains below. The giant glaciers encompassed the rim, looking majestic in the orange and yellow coats given to them by the morning sun. We climbed down eastwards along the crater rim to the top of the tourist track to Stella Point, then descending down steep scree to the Barafu Hut at 15,088 feet and onto the Mweka Hut at 10,170 feet, enjoying the increasing oxygen levels on the way down. We rested for a while at the start of the forest, then continued our descent to Mweka Village. Descending via an alternative route provided interesting variation to our climb, and distracted Steve and I from our relentless discussions of warm showers and cold beer. Our jeep was there to meet us and by 9pm we were back at the hotel in Moshi, exhausted. It had taken us just seven days to climb Meru and Kilimanjaro, and my legs were screaming at me for rest. My chest wall was tired, but we had completed the expedition in the time we had, and were both delighted. Our flight wasn't until 4pm, so the following morning we took a walk down the dusty track to Moshi centre. We stumbled across a young boy, busy painting fish on an old piece of dirty canvas. He couldn't speak English, but we conversed in jumbled French together and he recounted the story of why he was painting. He was the main bread-winner and provider in the family at twelve years of age. Both his mother and father had died from AIDS, and he also had the disease. He had a younger sister whom he looked after and tried to provide for, by selling his paintings. His tale was a sad one, but unlikely to be that unusual in the area, and of course one can never be too certain of the validity of stories like these. But I had been moved by his story. I bought several paintings from him, no doubt well above the local rate, and hoped that the money found its way to buying much needed provisions for the young lad and his sister.

Steve and I parted company at Heathrow airport, and I made my way back to Whitby by train. Clare met me at the train station, remarked on how dirty I looked and smelled (this despite the three showers I'd treated myself to the previous day), then dutifully kissed and hugged me, welcoming me home.

Africa hadn't left a good impression upon me. I had grown tired of the constant requests for money or gifts from people, tired of the warped bureaucracy demanding lubrication with currency at every opportunity, and tired of witnessing the disgraceful disparity between the haves and have-nots. I felt under surveillance wherever I had travelled in Tanzania, and had constantly been wary to never let my guard down. It had tired me out, in more ways than I can describe in words, and this had taken me by surprise. Clare sensed this, and I questioned whether I would ever travel to the African continent again. Amazingly, I did.

CLARE

The plan to travel to Carstensz had fallen through at the last minute and Ali found himself in the predicament of having leave but nowhere to go. We had intended to do Kilimanjaro together, to celebrate his success on completing the Seven, but this was the only option at the last minute. Ali was frustrated before he left for Africa, as he usually prepared for his climbs in meticulous detail months in advance. He would have read every description of the routes, know exactly what kit he required and have it packed, in a precise manner, many weeks before departure. This obsessive behaviour was probably the reason his previous expeditions had been so successful. I could tell by the brief conversations that Ali was not enjoying this trip and was trying to complete the task as quickly as possible. After Everest, Kilimanjaro did not challenge him enough physically and he was emotionally disturbed by the poverty and corruption of Africa. The young boy with AIDS had a profound, depressive effect on him. The realisation that much of the international aid, generously donated by many, was not reaching those in need made his frustration even worse. When he arrived home, he told me he would never go back to the African continent, but he would find himself there again two years later. On his second visit, he was better prepared and was able to see beyond the corruption and learned to admire the resilience and culture of the African people.

Chapter 7
Elbrus

March 28th 2007 was Shep's last day. He'd been failing for a month or two, and was finally ready to go. That morning he'd been unable to eat his food, just dribbling into his bowl, breathless from heart failure. I phoned the vet, who came out to the house. We had a long and difficult discussion, and decided that the kindest course of action was to put Shep down. I was heartbroken. He'd been with us for eleven years, since we got him from the rescue home, and although he'd been a little unpredictable at times had always remained loyal to Clare and me. He'd never really been any trouble, and had been a great companion, especially to Clare during my long absences. We buried him in the garden next to Newman, along with his favourite toy, a ball, and some chocolate, and said our final farewells.

Back at work, I'd not missed much. The trip had been a short one, but everyone was keen to hear of my tales and thumb through the pictures. We now had another summit to discuss in the talks that I gave around the area, and my thoughts soon returned to trying to complete the Seven Summits. I only had Mount Elbrus, the highest mountain on the European Continent at 18,510 feet, and Carstensz Pyramid to climb now, and felt that fulfilment of this dream was within my grasp. There were no expeditions leaving for Carstensz in the foreseeable future, due to the unrest in Papua and the difficulty gaining access to the mountain, so I decided to join an expedition to Elbrus with Alpine Ascents. Following several telephone conversations with their head office in Seattle, I was delighted to learn that Dave Morton was leading an Elbrus expedition in the summer of 2007. I'd climbed with Dave on Everest, and got on really well with him. He was a talented climber, a great teacher and instructor, and always put safety first. I spoke with Clare, spoke with the practice, and booked my flight to St Petersburg.

I'd always wanted to go to Russia, ever since studying the language at school. I found the alphabet, the culture, the history and its people fascinating, and really looked forward to my expedition to the country. The mountain itself stands at 18,841 feet, and is the highest mountain on the European continent. It is a large, double-coned volcano with twin summits that vary in height by 65 feet, and lies deep in the Caucasus Mountain Range. We would be linking up with a Russian guide as well for the climb, as the area was, and still remains, relatively volatile.

On arriving in St Petersburg, we met up at the hotel. It was great to catch up with Dave again, he'd just returned from another successful Everest expedition, and James, the friend who'd summited Denali with me, had reached the top with him. I was delighted by this, as James had remortgaged his house for the climb, and it was certainly going to be his one and only shot at Everest. I met up with the other team members, who had varying degrees of experience, and we settled in to our rooms. We planned to use the hotel as a base for a few days, which meant we didn't have to do too much carting around of our climbing gear from place to place. After supper on the first night, Dave gathered us together for a kit-check and to go over the itinerary. The following day or two would be sightseeing days around St Petersburg. Day four would be the flight to Mineralnye Vody, then we'd travel by bus to a small hotel in the Baskan Valley. The Baskan is famed for being a centre for mountaineering and skiing, being used by climbers from all over Russia to hone their skills before taking on the other mighty peaks around the world. Following a further gear-check the following day, we would begin our acclimatisation hikes into the Caucasus Range, first to 9,000 feet, then to 11,000 feet, gaining views of Elbrus, our main objective, on the way. Acclimatisation hikes that offer good views of the objective are great at focusing the mind on the job in hand. There was some anxiety amongst the less experienced members of our group and hopefully viewing the mountain for a couple of days on the hikes would help to dispel their fears. Day six, we would move to 'The Barrels'. These are, as the name suggests, giant barrels situated on Elbrus at 11,000 feet, forming permanent refuge to climbers on the mountain. Inside are crude bunk beds and storage areas, providing shelter from the elements and a place to rest. From the barrels, we would move to the Pruitt Hut, situated at about 14,000 feet, though location changes each year. This would be our high camp for the summit attempt, which would take twelve to fourteen hours. The itinerary had some flexibility for weather, as temperatures and wind can be brutal on the mountain, disappointing many with failed summit bids and capturing its fair share of permanent prisoners on its icy slopes.

My roommate for the first couple of nights was a chap from Canada, who'd recently had a successful ascent on Denali. An affable lad, he snored like a tank trying to run on the wrong fuel, but had a good sense of humour and we got on well. He looked a little out of shape as he dived into his bed under cover of the sidelight in the bedroom, but assured us all on many occasions that he'd trained hard for the trip.

Once at the mountain range, the first acclimatisation hikes went well, though my roommate was puffing and panting as we hiked up the hills. The purpose of these hikes was to stress the body into producing more red blood cells, thus making the summit climb easier as the body would be able to carry the extra oxygen that the muscles, lungs and brain would crave. Our final acclimatisation hike did not go to plan. Due to the threat from Chechen extremists, the UK Foreign and Commonwealth Office had advised against travel to the region for the past eight years. When descending from 11,000 feet, our hike was interrupted abruptly by a group of six men dressed in full army uniform. I wondered whether these were extremists. Several heated discussions took place between our Russian guide and the men. They just seemed to be starting to get along, when I decided, foolishly as it turned out, to move to a neighbouring rock to empty my now overflowing bladder. As I unzipped my fly, two rounds from a Kalashnikov semi-automatic rifle were let off over my head, signalling that the renegades were not pleased with my movement from the group. This shocked me enormously. I'd never been shot at before. Without finishing my task, I hurriedly redressed myself and moved back to the group, wondering what the next move would be. I should have guessed. Our guide asked us each for $50, which we would give the men as a 'contribution' to their cause. Everyone seemed quite happy to do this, especially me, if it meant no further firing of bullets above my head. Once this 'donation' had taken place, the mood changed completely. The army lads came over to us each in turn, shook our hands, and wished us a safe climb on the mountain. It was a little bizarre. I, in my best pidgin Russian, thanked the soldier who had fired over my head for curing my constipation. He laughed and we parted company on good terms, much to my relief.

The following day we moved up to the 'barrels'. They were every bit as primitive as I'd imagined. Giant domes, covered in tin-plating, housed ramshackle beds offering little support to our bodies. Food was cooked in a separate shed, and great care was taken by the team to wash and peel everything, to only drink water that we'd prepared, and to ensure all meat was hot when delivered to our plates. The food was bland but nutritious; I'd eaten a lot worse in Africa and parts of Nepal, so I tucked in happily to 'fuel my furnace'. The climb to the Pruitt hut was fairly straightforward, but we needed crampons and ice axes for the first time. Wisely, Dave had spent some time teaching the others ice-axe arrest technique and 'rest-stepping', a process by which the climber can make progress up a hill by resting the downhill leg between steps, thus preventing the build up of lactic acid in the muscles and easing the strain on the body. Holding an ice axe doesn't make you a climber, in the same way that holding a stethoscope doesn't make you a doctor. These skills are learnt over many years of hard work and determination.

The Pruitt Hut was a disaster just waiting to happen. Again bunk beds were the order of the day, though some of the group camped outside due to the claustrophobic nature of the accommodation. Inside the hut, eager cooking on open stoves filled the air with kerosene fumes, starting at ground level then rising to engulf those unfortunate enough to have 'bagged' a top bunk. It was impossible to sleep inside, so I set about preparing in advance for the following day's summit attempt. This relaxed me, as I took great comfort in knowing that everything was ready and that there would be no last-minute rushes out of camp with gear swinging from every available strap. Opening the door helped evacuate some of the noxious gas, but it was a cold and windy night outside, minus 15 or thereabouts, so people chose fume inhalation as the lesser of the two evils.

We set off for our summit attempt in the early hours, as usual, ensuring the safest passage across the snow. It was 2am, the night sky showering us with a fantastic view of the stars, the beams from our head-torches bobbing up and down on the black terrain ahead. There was the odd chunter from team members unable to get their crampons on properly or sacks done up. I'd been ready for a while, so assisted members of the team by tying crampons, checking harnesses, doing up rucksacks and so on. By 3am we were finally ready. A snowcat assisted our journey to the

Pastukov Rocks, carrying some of the climbers and gear. Once at the rocks, we organised ourselves into roped teams. Dave would head one team, our Russian guide another, and I would head the final team. I'd made sure my roommate was on my team, as I had some reservations about his level of fitness for the task and was really keen that he make it to the summit and back safely. I prodded the ground ahead with my ice axe to determine safe passage, aware that the terrain was littered with concealed crevasses. I was soon comfortable in the layering system I'd employed: a hat, balaclava, three layers under my Gortex jacket, thermals, two pairs of trousers, two pairs of gloves and high-altitude boots. By 6.30am, we were being treated to a wonderful dawn. The glow on the horizon signalling the beginning of the end of the freezing temperatures. The conical shadow of Elbrus was cast deep into the Caucasus Range by the sun coming up from the other side of the mountain, creating a spectacular backdrop to our climb. We stopped at 8am to replenish lost fluids, snack, and let our lungs and legs take a short but well-earned break. Everyone seemed in good spirits, and the other climbers on my rope team seemed to be coping well with the climb. By 9am, things had changed. My roommate had started to struggle. His movement was laboured, he was dragging his feet in the snow and ice, puffing and panting with every step. We were still a good couple of hours from the summit, and I had to employ all the motivation techniques I knew to get him to re-focus on the climb. We rested frequently from then on, constantly encouraging him to stay focussed, reminding him of the fun that lay in store after a successful climb, but all the time being wary of his condition. It's a fine line sometimes between helping a colleague achieve their dreams and ambitions, and letting someone move beyond their safe limits on that particular day and at that particular time. I watched him carefully and felt sure that the tiredness and general lethargy was more mental than physical. He was alert when I talked to him, and showed no signs of either pulmonary or cerebral oedema. At 10.40am, we took the last few steps up to the summit of Elbrus together, and the fatigue was forgotten as we took in the ice blue sky clear of any storm clouds, and the horizon peppered with mountaintops as far as the eye could see. In the distance was a spectacular view of Ushba, considered the Matterhorn of the region, with its giant towering twin peaks joined by a rocky saddle. The whole team had made it to the summit, which was fantastic. I'd been lucky again, despite poor weather forecasts, a summit day had presented itself that was clear, windless and relatively straightforward, and this was now the sixth continent on which I had made it to the highest possible point. I was well aware that fortune had shone upon me in that all six had been reached at the first attempt. Climbers often spend many, many years to get to the point that I had in four years, and I felt privileged to be in the position that I was. All that remained between completing the coveted 'Seven Summits' and my current position was a safe descent from Elbrus, then a trip to the elusive Carstensz Pyramid in Indonesia.

Everyone descended safely, and a couple of days later we were back at the hotel. We celebrated in fine style with an enormous barbeque of local meats – though I didn't want to inquire as to which beasts they had come from – salads, wine and beer. The mood was great. We took a brief trip by four-wheel drive to a local outdoor market to make some purchases and experience some of the local culture. An experience it certainly was. I walked through the dusty passages between the stalls, morbidly curious as the vendors butchered live animals for the clients lining up in an orderly fashion holding their currency. Sheep, chickens, goats, their blood spilling from the bucket placed at the side of their necks where the knife had cut, and running onto the sandy dirt of the street. Their legs kicked and twitched randomly, speeding the bleeding process as the creatures scuttled along the path towards their fate. Skins from many different animals were on sale, various fruits, and leather goods sewn by the locals at the market. Thick, acrid, re-smoked tobacco fumes filled the air, with the smell of warm iron from the buckets of blood, leaving a taste of rancid coffee and old metal filings in my mouth. Most of what I saw made me feel uneasy, but this was their world, and this was how they lived.

On arrival at the airport for our departure, my room mate expressed his thanks for our time on the climb, and asked me to keep an eye out for the wine he'd send me over from his home town. I'm still keeping both eyes open for it. It had been a pleasure to see him realise another dream of his, and helping him along had given me greater confidence on the hill. Dave and I parted company once more, knowing that we'd meet up again soon.

CLARE

Ali had studied Russian at school and had looked forward to this trip, not only for the climbing but also to experience some of the culture. I would have gone, but was at home studying for my exit exam to become a consultant surgeon the following week. The pictures of the churches and architecture of St Petersburg were amazing and we plan to go back there together in the future. My husband and my mother, Peggy, have always had a tempestuous relationship but are really very fond of each other. Ali had visited a beautiful church and had bought Peggy a wooden idol depicting Our Lady of Tenderness holding the infant Jesus. Ali had no idea that that Peggy always prayed to Our Lady of Tenderness to protect her children, as she is the patron saint of families. I think this was the favourite present Peggy ever received and it sits on her bedside table to this day.

Chapter 8
Carstensz Pyramid

The summer of 2007 was a very busy one at the practice. Some of the partners had not been well, the tourist season seemed to extend well into October, and rest and recreation appeared to be a luxury. Clare and I got out for plenty of early morning runs on the beach and along the old railway line with the dogs. I spent most of the autumn working towards my expedition to Carstensz Pyramid. Timing would be important, just long enough from Elbrus to let Clare feel she'd seen me in 2007, yet short enough to keep my climbing skills honed. I was desperately keen to complete the Seven, but no teams seemed to be preparing for Carstensz, until I finally got a positive email from Mountain Trip, a company that I'd climbed with before as part of the climb on Denali. They were putting together a team in November 2007, and had asked me if I'd like to join. I didn't hesitate in accepting, and after several meals out to fancy restaurants, and cleaning out the flower shop on more than one occasion, Clare came on board. So rarely do teams go to this region that it was likely that I'd only get one shot at the climb. I was aware that the summit rate was low, mainly due to the mountain's inaccessibility and to local political unrest. Foreign Office advice was again strongly against travelling to this region, but on the balance of risk and the likelihood of another team going to the region, I decided it was worth it.

Out of the blue, I got an email from Chris, with whom I had stood on top of Mount Everest. He was going on the climb too, and we were both delighted that we'd be able to catch up with each other again. We emailed each other frequently before departure, and it was obvious we were both completely psyched up for the climb and the difficulties that lay ahead. We would leave for Carstensz in November 2007.

The next few months were manic. The running season was a productive one: I managed to run six full marathons and countless half marathons in preparation for the climb. I wanted to join the '100 marathons' club, and was nearly half way there. The running was great to keep me fit and focussed for upcoming climbs, and my running partners Freda, Clare, Kevin, Steve and Paul all enjoyed the same distance races as myself. As a group, we got along really well. Runners are generally an odd bunch, usually middle-aged, invariably fit, and unreservedly fixated about their bowels, and this group was no exception. Often we'd pass around the Lomotil (a drug used in the treatment of diarrhoea) the day before race day to ensure the bowel had no desire to open during the race. October of that year was particularly busy. Some of us went over to the Chicago Marathon, one firmly fixed in our calendar year on year. The following weekend I did another marathon on the Saturday in London, and then a half marathon on the Sunday.

November came round all too soon for Clare. She didn't seem too happy at me getting ready for another expedition so soon after the last, but deep down she understood that my dream of completing the Seven Summits was now within touching distance. She had read the Foreign Office advice, and questioned me frequently on it. I was in regular contact with Bill, who was to guide the trip, and he was confident that all the necessary cogs had been greased to make the trip run smoothly. I departed two days after my birthday, on November 19th, Clare once again ferrying me to the airport. We had arranged to meet up at a hotel in Bali, and the team comprised nine climbers. It was quite a big team due to the allure of a climb on Carstensz. Many teams had gone over to try and climb it, but very few had been successful, in fact, hardly anyone has climbed it since the first ascent in 1961. The trip would be full of uncertainty. In Bali, Bill went over the proposed itinerary. We planned to fly over the Freeport Mine by Russian helicopter to get to base camp, which is the most desirable access method. The Freeport Mine is the largest gold mine and third largest copper mine in the world. The cost of building the mine was US$3 billion, and it employs nineteen thousand five hundred people. The mine authorities guard the mine vigorously, and anyone caught trespassing there is dealt with extremely firmly. Climbers have been imprisoned for long periods of time when caught on the property. This partially acts as a deterrent to other climbers accessing the mine by going through it, and also serves to let the authorities demonstrate their purpose to the locals. The helicopter option suited us well, avoiding travel through the mine. We planned to fly to Timika the following day, and from there take the helicopters to base camp. We had set aside three days for the summit attempt, and took time to study the route. It would involve scrambling and rock climbing up the North Face, fixing some rope to help us on the route. From there, we would descend and ascend three notched areas, the first of which is a free-hanging section requiring a technique known as Tyrolean Traverse, or dragging yourself along a rope fixed between two points of rock with nothing but air underneath you. Descent from the summit would be by the same route.

The flight to Timika was only a couple of hours from Bali. We stayed the first night at an insect-ridden shanty lodge that provided little more than a roof over our heads. The locals were extremely interested in our presence, pacing around outside our rooms, peering through the bare windows and following us closely as we moved between each other's rooms. Many of them were armed with knives and guns, making the team feel uneasy. We hired some local armed guards to stand by at the gates of the 'hotel' to deter any trouble, and resigned ourselves to a disturbed night. After dark my rest was constantly interrupted by insects flying close to my ears and distant gunfire coming from the villages. I wanted to get out of there as fast as possible. I spent most of the night on and off the satellite phone to Clare, most definitely more for my comfort than hers. I just had a bad feeling about the place, the climb and our current situation, and Clare could sense it in my voice. This, of course, worried her; she in turn phoned the Mountain Trip HQ in America, who were able to tell her absolutely nothing at all.

We gathered together in one room in the morning, where Bill delivered the bad news. Unfortunately the Russian pilots, along with their helicopters, had found more productive work elsewhere, and had decided not to take us to the mountain, but instead to leave with our money. They had kindly intimated that they might be able to come back 'at some stage in the future' to give us a ride, if we'd like to wait until then. This created many problems. We had no alternative plan for getting to base camp, we could not wait too many days as people had commitments at home, and none of us wanted to spend any more time staying in Timika. The highest peak on the Australasian Continent was living up to its elusive reputation, and we weren't even anywhere close to our target region yet. Walking to the Surinam Mountain Range would not be possible from where we were, and now that the helicopter flights from Wamena were out of the question, we were only left with one option – to go through the mine. The team talked for hours about this possibility, as it would involve gaining illegal and dangerous access, not something that any of us relished. We thought long and hard, and eventually the team decided to go for it. The process would involve travelling via one of the mine transport buses, dressed as miners, and lying on the floor hiding at the frequent checkpoints through the mine. Travel to the bus would be in the back of an army truck, and transport from the bus at the other side of the mine would be by four-wheel drives. We were to remain silent at all times. On the bus would be security soldiers, armed, and any irregular behaviour would be dealt with 'in the appropriate manner'. I was not sure what that meant, but didn't ask, deciding it would be better just to maintain appropriate behaviour at all times! As the security men and drivers all had to be bribed, this would take care of the rest of the teams' finances. It also put the accepters of the bribes at great risk. Wages in the area were pitiful, and the money we were prepared to pay would have been almost six months' salary to these people, but they were taking an incalculable risk by offering to be part of the plan. They would not want to get caught assisting us, under any circumstances.

We left the village at 11pm, for our rendezvous with the army truck at midnight. Inside the truck was sweltering, with almost 100% humidity and temperatures close to 90 degrees. We sat and waited nervously, while many conversations in local dialect took place outside, the voices occasionally rising and feet stamping on the ground. We were totally at the mercy of these locals, and the whole situation was very alien to us all. After an hour or so, the lorry finally moved off with us in the back. We were due to meet up with the bus on the outskirts of the mine at about 2am, and would transfer vehicles at the army barracks undercover, being guided from vehicle to vehicle only by those aware of our presence and whose pockets had been filled beforehand.

Transfer to the bus went without a hitch. Once on the bus, we all duly put on our miners hats and jackets, and awaited instructions. 'At each checkpoint, you will act asleep – lie down so not seen' came the clear instruction from the Commandant at the front of the bus. 'Lay still, do not move, do not talk'. On each side of a climber a security guard was situated, armed of course, to ensure that these instructions were carried out. The boy next to me must have been no older than sixteen, dressed in his army uniform, looking almost as nervous as me, the sweat running down the barrel of his semi-automatic rifle and onto my thigh, creating a small damp patch that seeped through my trousers. The journey through the mine took about five hours, and it was the worst five hours of my life. My heart pounded as the adrenaline rushed blood into my head, 'whoooshing' between my ears, just waiting for the nervous young boy resting his rifle on me to jump and pull the trigger. It was horrible, made all the worse by the enforced blackout in the bus. At every checkpoint the Commandant would shout 'Sleep' loudly from the front, and the climbing team would lie down and dare not move a muscle. There must have been fifteen checkpoints going through the mine, and at each one I thought, 'Is this it? Is this where we are caught, imprisoned, and forgotten about?' There was a small altercation between the Commandant and a policeman at one checkpoint, but it was resolved by the exchange of a handful of dollars and eventually we were through. We'd passed deep mineshafts, rubble roads and sand to get to the other side of the mine, and my only thoughts at that point were 'bloody hell, we have to go through all of that again on the way back'. Once through the mine, we were hustled into three four-wheel drive vehicles, again dressed as miners, and transported to the mountain. Had I known what it would involve, I might have elected to climb Kosciuszko instead, regarded by a few as one of the Seven Summits and infinitely easier to get to and climb than Carstensz.

We were finally there. A short trek up the hill and we set up base camp on Carstensz, by the side of a large lake. It felt good to be out of the lorry-bus-truck scenario, and now we could set our sights on the task ahead. This climb was different from the others, a rock climb of moderate difficulty, requiring a strength and skill that other big climbs don't always need. Base camp gave us all a little time to catch our breath after the traumas of the previous couple of days. I remember thinking to myself that if the climb and return journey were successful, then I would definitely be treating myself to a decent hotel and fine cuisine in Bali.

Day two on the mountain consisted mainly of ferrying our gear up the hill from base camp to camp 1. From here, when rested and weather permitting, we would mount our summit bid. The trek between the camps was along a narrow, rocky path. We were carrying big loads, and some of us offered to do a double-carry, returning from camp 1 to base camp to carry another load up the hill. I was pretty relaxed about doing this, as the first carry hadn't tired me and I really needed to refocus my mind after the ordeal of the journey. I was also acutely aware that the same journey would have to be completed in reverse when we'd summited the mountain, and this was an experience that I was not looking forward to.

Camp 1 was at approximately 13,780 feet, and was situated by another lake. The day was a calm one and the weather was gracious in its co-operation, a still and peaceful environment, the lake water motionless and creating a perfect reflection of the rock faces on the opposite side. I took time after the carries to go over to the giant wall of rock at the base of the mountain and feel it. The harsh limestone was cold and sharp, yet comforting in the same way that feet feel when correctly positioned in a well-fitting ski boot. There appeared to be plenty of good holds on the rock, which felt grippy. The area is known for its rains, and the rock felt saturated. Waterfalls flung themselves haphazardly over the face from up high, crashing to their conclusions many feet below. I could just about make out the line of the route to the summit, along several vertical and horizontal cracks in the wall, between the waterfalls and huge overhangs of unclimbable rock. I did not underestimate the challenge that lay ahead. My focus turned to the possibility of completing the Seven Summits.

After selecting a suitable area to be the platform for my tent that night, I joined the others in our makeshift mess to eat and talk strategy. As it would be a rope climb, we decided to take some time the following day going over knots, rope work, abseiling and rappelling, all the tools and techniques that we would be using on the climb itself. Then, if the weather was kind to us, we would attempt to go to the summit the following day. We had a deadline to meet: in three days time, at 10pm, our four-wheel drive vehicles would be waiting for us at the foot of the hill, to transport us back to the bus for getting through the mine. The vehicles would only wait for us for two hours. We had to be there, otherwise we had no way of getting home. By now, I was under no illusion as to why Carstensz Pyramid was by far the most elusive of the Seven. Logistically, the expedition planning was bordering on impossible. With this knowledge and our bellies full from the hot soup and stew that we'd consumed, we retired to our tents for some well-earned rest and relaxation.

I always missed Clare and the dogs when I was away, but even more so on this trip due to the dangers that had confronted us. I find it relatively straightforward having to deal with the complexities of mountain weather, equipment, avalanches, heat and supplies, but bring untested communities and authorities into the equation and the situation is much more volatile.

I tried to sleep, listening to various tunes and trying to settle, but the previous day's activities weighed heavily on my mind. I feared for the journey back, and felt uncomfortable at the pressure of having to be back at the foot of the mountain at a precise time to make that journey. It all went against the ethos of why I go on expeditions. There are generally no time limits, and the focus is on keeping warm, keeping healthy, and climbing safely... but not here.

The following day we awoke to a beautiful morning. The rains that had drowned our campsite overnight had subsided, and as I unzipped the front of my tent the sun was strong. I got myself together in the tent, and then went out for a stretch and stroll around camp. The lake looked swollen with the rains. Some of the other team members were up and starting to lay their climbing clothes over the top of their tents to dry out. I chatted a while with Chris, then we got down to the business of the day, practising the techniques that we'd all be needing the next day on the climb. It was clear that the skill mix was varied; some of the team were proficient, others had to be taught almost from first principles, but by early evening everyone seemed happy with what they would be expected to do. That night we went over the route to the top once more, the guides referring to their notes as neither had climbed Carstensz before. We made plans to leave the following morning at around 3am, to give us a full day on the climb. We anticipated that it would take at least twelve to fourteen hours to accomplish the route, and decided we had to be off the mountain and back at camp by nightfall.

Yet another restless night followed, and by 1am I was up inside my tent, packing my rucksack and preparing for the day ahead. I was not going to leave the tent at 3am in a rush. The climb itself was likely to be difficult, and I did not want to add to my stress levels by wondering which key item of equipment I'd forgotten to bring in my hasty exit. By 2.30am everything was ready. My water bottles were full and my sack packed, with several pairs of gloves positioned in the top as the rock and multiple rappelling and abseiling would probably tear them to shreds. The weather was co-operative again, no rain and about 8 degrees Celsius. The team gathered in the mess tent at 3am, and set off up the trail to the foot of the climb. By 5am we were well up the rock face. The climbing was hard, vertical in places and down to 45 degrees in others. Some parts required me to hold my nerve as I scrambled from foothold to handhold in the dark, reaching the full length of my torso to secure safety, aware of the free air that surrounded the tiny perch I was on. Most of us struggled in the dark, but we all waited for each other, helped where we could, and climbed very much as a team. There was a quiet awareness and realisation that we were, in fact, exceptionally lucky to have gained access to the mountain; none of us wanted to go home without seeing the summit as we would be unlikely to get the chance to return to the region. As dawn broke and I switched my head torch off, my range of vision turned from the narrow cylinder of light thrown directly in front of me to a wonderful panoramic landscape. Huge limestone cliffs and mountains, jagged tops like sharks' teeth serrated between each ravine. Fresh snow lay around us from 12,000 feet upwards, reminding us of the previous night's rainfall lower down the elevations at camp 1. In daylight, the climbing became more straight-forward. The hand and footholds suddenly became easier to find and the route ahead less complex. The views were magnificent, distracting me from the metalwork that hung from my harness and reminding me why I craved these environments so much. The moves between rope pitches became smooth, and the team gathered pace towards the Tyrolean Traverse. There would be no room for error at this point, and we all knew that success here would be likely to lead to a successful summit.

Arriving at the traverse signalled the start of an anxious hour for the group. Old rope lay strewn between the two peaks, and access to the other side to place new rope down for the team to cross on meant that one climber would have to risk traversing on the old rope. With wind chafing the old corroded rope against the rock, the likelihood of a rope fouling and breaking becomes unacceptably high, still the rope seemed in reasonable condition on our side, so we elected to give it a try. Bill was the first to go over. We secured him as safely as we could to what we had available, then off he went across the old rope traverse. He was an experienced climber and solid guide, and after ten minutes or so had safely reached the other side with the fresh rope. This was swiftly secured between the two peaks and the rest of the team began to make their way across the gorge. Mid-way across I took a moment from hauling myself and my rucksack along the line, to look around. The drop beneath me was immense, as was the exposure of the position, but the views were captivating. Brown and grey peaks filled my vision, dusted with snow on their caps, filling in their cracks and imperfections so most faces looked topographically the same.

The sun shone down on the valleys below, providing contrast with greens and yellows coating the lower mountainsides and deeper ravines, and on the waterfalls coursing their way down towards the lakes. Once over to the other side of the traverse, I couldn't help but notice the condition of the rope along which Bill had pulled himself. It had been damaged by exposure and chafed almost entirely through. 'Good job Bill's not a fatty,' I thought to myself, 'else we'd be a man short on the team now.' Bill was less amused when he saw the part-broken rope on which he'd risked his life a few moments earlier.

By 11am, we were nearing the summit. Chris and I were climbing in tandem, and after another couple of narrow ridges and exposed passages, we rounded a rock to be greeted with the view of two of the team celebrating on the top. As we made our way towards them, I got a lump in my throat. I felt pretty choked that this was it, the final few footsteps towards the summit of my seventh of the Seven Summits. Chris and I put our arms around each other at the top, as we'd done on the summit of Everest eighteen months before. A Russian team who had reached the top of the mountain previously had left a logbook inside a metal container, which we all signed. We shook hands with each other, then stopped for a few photos. I had scribbled 'That's No.7!' on a piece of A4 paper in the hope that I could unfurl it on the summit – and so I did. Once again I reminded myself that most mountain deaths occur during the descent, and after a brief stop on the top we set off for camp 1. By 2pm, the rains started, and boy did it rain. It absolutely threw it down, coming from what appeared to be every direction, mixed with hail and snow, driving into any place that wasn't completely protected by Gore-Tex. I was glad that I'd prepared for two changes of gloves; my hands were wet and frozen and my gloves torn. Twice I changed them, and each time they met the same fate, getting ripped and burnt to pieces on the abseiling sections, hundreds of feet at a time. In the torrential rains, getting down proved tougher than expected for everyone. The ropes and our clothes were drenched, and nightfall arrived sooner than anticipated.

The last hour of climbing down was one of the longest hours I'd spent on any climb, my tiredness akin to that on the descent from Aconcagua. Every muscle ached and my eyes hurt from squinting through the freezing rain. My fingers were numb with cold, my fingernails cracked and broken from the splintering rock and my feet freezing in my boots. It was 7pm by the time we all reached the safety of camp. There was barely enough time to eat, drink, change into dry clothes, pack up and descend to our meeting point with the vehicles, and we were all exhausted. However, we knew that there were no options other than the plan we had, so we set about clearing camp. The carry down had me falling over more than once. The loads were heavy, sixty pounds or more; my legs had little more to give and the path was uneven. Nightfall had also arrived and my head torch was desperately trying to put out its last beam of light from the fading batteries. We were all aware of the tight timescale for the descent, and hurried as best we could for fear of abandonment on the mountain. The four-wheel drive vehicles were where they said they would be, and hurriedly they ushered us into the back. We were an hour behind schedule but they had decided to wait for ninety minutes – we'd just made it. I didn't even have time to start to get worried about the illegal journey through the mine that lay ahead, choosing instead to flop onto my rucksack and await instructions from the armed driver.

Two hours later, the vehicles arrived at our rendezvous with the bus that would take us through the mine. We were hastily moved from the vehicles to a 'holding room', given some inedible food, told not to drink the water, and then left for what seemed like an eternity. I looked around the room at the team; we all looked totally shattered. Our clothing was drenched and filthy from the mountain, our boots clogged with muck and grime, climbing jackets ripped from snagging on the limestone, fingers cut and chins unshaven. All eyes were shut while we waited for instructions, everyone seemingly unshaken by our precarious position in that solitary room. Eventually, the Commandant arrived. He went over instructions on 'you will look asleep' again in the bus, warned us all to be silent at all times, and we boarded our bus. The drive back through the mines went through fewer checkpoints than on the way in. We were stopped and boarded once by police or security guards; again money changed hands, then we were on our way again. I guessed that if we had been caught by a less 'helpful' official, they would probably want us on our way and off their property anyway; as we had now completed the climb, we had little to lose. Seven hours of being tossed around on metal seats in a bus with no suspension, in the dark, soon passed, and we arrived back in the village. Given the locals' unhealthy interest in our presence, we elected to try for the first flight out to get back to Bali. We were all desperate to leave this inhospitable environment, and the relief was palpable when, the following morning, we boarded the aircraft.

Back at the hotel in Bali we started to relax, consuming cocktails, taking hot showers, and swimming in the pool. I was keen to get home to see Clare, Chino and Coco, to get back to some normality of routine. This trip had taken it out of me, both physically and mentally, and I was ready to see home again. The team split away from the hotel at intervals, Chris and I planning to catch up when I was next in San Francisco seeing my sister-in-law and her husband, and the expedition came to its end. What a trip it had been. It had involved everything – political tension, theft, smuggling, disappointment, exposure, beauty, unbelievable weather patterns and stress beyond belief, but we had succeeded in our aim of climbing the highest mountain on the Oceanic Continent, and for that we were all very relieved.

It was the end of my Seven Summits challenge; I had climbed them all without having to return to any of them. Four years and three hundred and four days after standing on top of Aconcagua, the challenge was over. The time that it had taken me was by no means a record, but I knew of no other climbers who had been fortunate enough to have summited all seven at the first attempt. I felt complete, at last, and I now had the full set of seven miniature black china cats from my parents, having received one prior to each of the climbs in my quest to climb the Seven Summits.

Clare and I shared another emotional reunion at the airport. Through patchy telephone conversations she had been aware of how precarious our situation had been on this climb. She was pleased to have me back in her arms, and was both relieved and proud that this Seven Summits adventure had reached its finale. The dogs were happy to have their alpha dog back in the pack, and I was welcomed with the usual array of wet tongues, barks and toys being dropped at my feet. Christmas wasn't far away now, and I sensed that they knew they would soon be begging for a nibble of one of Shirley's famous mince pies. This climb had been by far the most difficult of the Seven Summits for me, and I was delighted to have succeeded on it. It remains the climb that satisfied me the most. It was a one-off, and leaves me in no doubt why some people would prefer to claim Kosciuszko (the highest point in Australia, at 7,313 feet) as the seventh summit, and why only a fraction of those people who have stood on the summit of Mount Everest have been fortunate enough to see the world from the summit of the highest mountain in Oceania. Had I had any idea that climbing Carstensz would involve the events that had unfolded when we were there, then I, too, might have been lured to Kosciuszko instead. But then again... maybe not.

In a quiet moment of lucidity, I reflected on the cost of this adventure to the top of the Seven Summits. Without any sponsorship, it cost somewhere in the region of £200,000, and that is assuming that all are successfully summited at the first attempt. I had always raised the finances for the climbs from "extra" work outside our normal combined work income, and that had taken its toll. Working many, many nights on-call, away from Clare, sleeping on a roll mat in between answering phonecalls from worried patients and visiting them in their homes between 11pm and 8am had been hard work. Had it been worth all those nights away from home, burning all that midnight oil? Well, I think so, but it caused unrest at home on many occasions. If I hadn't had the backing and understanding of a wife trying to run her own busy career, then the costs would have been much greater for sure. St Catherine's Hospice has certainly benefited from the fundraising that the marathons and climbs have brought, with over £25,000 raised so far, and that in itself brings me a great deal of pride. I continue to raise funds for them now, and they will remain the focus of any future expeditions that present the opportunity for fund-raising.

CLARE

Ali was away to Carstensz and spent the first few days in Bali. I was really jealous! Peggy had come down to help with the dogs and I was enjoying her company greatly. I came home early one afternoon to find Peggy and our friend Elaine in the kitchen and I could tell something was wrong immediately. I had insisted that Ali hire a satellite phone to take on all his trips, to ensure that he always had a means of contacting home. I knew he had tried to call my mobile a couple of times that day, but I had been stuck in the operating theatre where there was no reception. Mum asked me if I had spoken to Ali. I told her I had missed him a couple of times. She told me that she'd had a brief conversation with him that day and that he sounded frightened. I love my mother dearly but she can overstate things at times and I did not take it too seriously. Within the hour, Ali phoned home again and I could hear the fear in his voice. For the second time, I was truly concerned about his safety and did not know what to do with myself. I asked him a number of questions to try and establish what was going on, but he seemed unable to answer me fully, as if someone was stopping him from answering. When we lost our connection, I called the Mountain Trip office in America immediately to try and get some information. This was the first and only time I ever phoned an expedition company. It was a complete waste of time. They did not have any organised system of contact and wanted me to keep them informed of developments!

The next two weeks were difficult. I was restless, found it hard to concentrate on my work and was glad when Ali left Papua New Guinea. The relief that he'd completed the Seven Summits was overwhelming, but the joy I felt for Ali and his incredible achievement was tainted by the effect this climb had had on us at home. When I think back on all his journeys, I am so thankful that I never had a call informing me that he had been injured, or worse still, killed on a mountain. The helplessness that you feel when your husband is on another continent and far from help is hard to live with. We were lucky, but many families have to deal with that kind of tragedy every year. They are the true heroes of the mountaineering world.

Chapter 9
Timbuktu

Life during the day got back to normal after a couple of weeks, but nights were a problem when I first returned home from the Carstensz trip. I could not rest properly, reminding myself constantly of the trip through the mine, the locals rampaging outside the ramshackle hotel rooms, and the sound of gunfire in the distance in the villages. It had all been very unnerving, and it took some time to recede from my thoughts. Practice life was busy; the Christmas and New Year period always was, with everyone wanting to be well for the holidays. With both of our parents still enjoying good health but not getting any younger, we always tried to visit one or both sets at this time of year.

Days, weeks and months soon passed, and Clare sensed that I was becoming restless again. Now the Seven Summits challenge was complete, I started looking at other climbs to get involved in, particularly K2. This had been a bone of contention between myself and Clare for several years. K2 is well-known for its difficulties and poor summit rate, as well as high mortality rates, with one in three of all of those who summit dying on the descent. For Clare, these statistics were too risky, and I knew that for once there could be real problems if I ignored her fears, even though I regarded it as a real mountaineer's mountain. The year I had been thinking of going turned out to be a disastrous one on the mountain, with the upper slopes of K2 claiming the lives of eleven of the eighteen climbers attempting to summit. This was definitely a climb that I would leave, for now.

Clare, sensing my 'itchy feet' one day in the summer, advised me in her own inimitable and apposite way, 'You spend so much time away from home, I don't know why you don't just go to Timbuktu.' And that was it. A plan started to hatch. I've had a long-time love affair with motorcycles, I'm fascinated by their mechanics, love the thrill of riding, and enjoy the bond that bikers share with each other and their machines. So, why not take one to Timbuktu and back? Then, out of the blue, I heard that

Nick Sanders, a motorcycle journalist, philosopher and eccentric from the south of England, was running a trip through Africa and was looking for motorcyclists with a 'strong sense of adventure' to join him. Nick and I talked on the phone, I went over the preliminary plans with him, and I was in. It was simple, on paper. Twelve thousand five hundred miles from Whitby to Timbuktu, via France, Spain, Morocco, Western Sahara, Mauritania and Mali, then back to Whitby, all within twenty-six days. The trip would require long days of four to five hundred miles on tarmac, broken road and dust tracks leading to the Sahara, then several hundred miles off piste into the desert. It would have all the elements that my climbing expeditions brought to my life, namely an itinerary requiring careful planning, no elements of certainty, a strong objective, travel, and most of all adventure. I needed to be involved in a motorcycle adventure. They had been such an important part of my life that this would tick all the right boxes. I talked through the plans with Clare, who was relaxed about the trip – after all, this was not K2 – and started gathering my kit together again in our spare bedroom.

Motorcycle selection for the task that lay ahead proved easy. For years I've had a great relationship with York Suzuki, a motorcycle business near where I live. I wanted to take one of their bikes, with their logos on the machine, and if successful hoped to generate some interest in their motorcycles, to give something back to the family-owned business that had been so good to me over the years. I talked at length with Goose, the owner of the shop, and we settled on a new, off-road styled Suzuki, which we would modify extensively to cope with the task that lay ahead. It would need to be reliable, economical, and above all completely robust and hopefully almost unbreakable.

It took five months to prepare the bike and, with the departure date set at February 2nd from the South of England, it was only completed mid-January. I took it for an extended test run to see my parents and back, a round trip of five hundred miles, and all seemed well. Following my climbing ethos of travelling as light as possible, I settled for two aluminium panniers and one of my climbing duffel bags to carry all essentials. The bike was ready, and so was I. On February 1st 2009 I left Whitby; it was snowing hard. I headed for my parents house, where I would spend the night, then set off for Portsmouth the following day, to catch the ferry to France.

The morning was bitterly cold. The snow had settled on the ground from the night before and was still falling heavily. I left my parents' house at 6am, giving myself six hours to the ferry terminal, where I planned to meet up with the other members of the team. My motorcycle was ready for the rigours of sand dunes, anticipated crashes, infrequent petrol stops and long periods in the saddle, along with safety equipment such as satellite navigation and auxiliary power sockets to charge communication devices. I'd gathered a reasonable supply of spares together for the trip, such as replacement tyres, puncture repair kits, spare brake pads, oil, spare filters and suchlike, and packed it all into two metal panniers, tank bag and duffel, with the spare tyres strapped behind me on the pillion seat. The ride to Portsmouth was miserable, with heavy snowfall and low visibility on the road, made worse by high winds throwing the bike viciously from side to side on the carriageway as its heavy load doubled as a sail, constantly catching large gusts of wind. I made it to Portsmouth in good time, partly helped by nurturing my fingers and chest in various heated garments that I plugged into the bike. I'd learnt a long time ago that to fail because of poor planning is a waste of everyone's time and effort.

The first team member I met up with at Portsmouth was Steve. We immediately hit it off as we were riding the same make of bike. It turned out that Steve was a fanatic about this particular type of motorcycle, and had owned them for many years. He helped run an international club devoted to the Suzuki DL 650, and spent a comfortable hour or two telling me of all their merits. He was a nice guy, enthusiastic about the trip, and described it as his trip of a lifetime. He'd saved for it over a few years, and was excited about what lay ahead. The most important part of any successful expedition where people spend long periods of time unsupervised is the development of a working 'buddy-system'. This allows both of the members to look out for each other along the way, and has proved valuable to me on many occasions in the mountains. We decided to buddy each other for the trip, and set about going over our route maps together. The snow fell relentlessly outside the ferry terminal as other team members gradually arrived. Finally, Nick, our facilitator, turned up in a pick-up for carrying broken bikes, with his girlfriend Caroline, a retired (though still young) GP, and we boarded the ferry. We settled in to our overnight cabins, and then reconvened in the snack bar to check the itinerary.

'This isn't The World Of BMW's Luxury Tour', was Nick's opening gambit, a phrase he'd repeat on many occasions during the ensuing weeks. Clearly this was a low-budget operation set up to assist broad-minded and adventurous motorcyclists achieve riding ambitions, its success largely depending on the inspiration and drive of the individuals themselves. This suited me fine. I was happy to look after myself in most types of situation, had a reasonable command of the French language used in many parts of Africa, and liked the idea of being largely unassisted. It adds to the sense of achievement when a trip ends sucessfully.

The remainder of the team were; a retired Australian whose son had ridden to Timbuktu the year before, friends with another Australian who'd brought his girlfriend on the back of his KTM motorcycle; a couple from Yorkshire, near where I lived, on a BMW; a retired policeman on a Yamaha, and Steve and I. There was another lad who hadn't made the ferry, Andy, who'd unfortunately come off his Honda in the snow on the way. He'd hopefully be catching up with us in France.

Nick and Caroline had jotted down an outline of the route. A brief look through had some of the team raising their eyebrows. An average of four hundred miles a day, sometimes more, was certainly food for thought. I was unsure why there should have been any concern, after all, the return journey to Timbuktu was twelve thousand five hundred miles, and we had twenty-five days for the trip, there was no magic in the figures. Once at Caen, after a few hours of sleep, we disembarked with our bikes and headed south. It was still snowing hard, and the KTM rider was regretting only having brought summer gloves for the trip, thinking maybe that the weather would be reminiscent of the Sahara all the way from England to Africa, instead of the sub-zero temperatures we were now experiencing. Snow or sun, we still had to make strong headway towards Biarritz in Southern France. I lent him my spare winter riding gloves to prevent him getting frostbite, and we headed off. The journey was cold and wet, with no sun or subsequent rising of the temperature. Andy had joined us in southern France, catching up from his earlier fall on the way to Portsmouth. With the distances that we were doing each day, I was utterly amazed that he'd caught us up.

It turned out he had ridden two eighteen-hour days to reach us, but he and his bike looked well. An army man by profession, Andy had a keen interest in photography and often stopped en route to capture images to accompany the stories at a later date. His Honda wore the battle scars of the accident well, and he was determined to get his bike to the mystical city of Timbuktu and back. His grandmother had left him some money to help finance the trip, and I could tell by his account of events leading up to the departure that this was his lifetime ambition. I really hoped he'd make it.

Steve and I kept close on the road, stopping every hundred miles to rest our eyes from the effect of snow flurries dancing in front of our faces. The white dots become hypnotic after a short while, inducing fatigue and risking avoidable accidents. We made it to our destination by 10pm, and found the overnight accommodation that Nick had arranged. It was a simple hostel, but fit for its purpose of giving us warmth, food, and a place to dry some clothes and get some sleep. The bike was averaging fifty miles to a gallon, more than acceptable from an average speed of 60mph for ten hours. The following day was more of the same, snow, rain, cold and tarmac. Another four hundred and fifty miles saw us journey deep into Spain, stopping overnight just outside Madrid. Sleep was intermittent when covering these sort of distances. Initially, when I lay down exhausted, my body was desperate for rest but not for sleep. I could still feel the vibration of the road under the balls of my feet and still see the snow in front of my eyes. Eventually I would fall asleep while trying to count the individual snowflakes as my eyes remained closed. Then, all too soon, my alarm would fire off in my ear, declaring that it was time to get up, pack up the bike, and head off again towards the African continent.

Day 3 we headed from Madrid towards Algeciras, to get the ferry to Tangiers. I couldn't believe it: we were in Southern Spain in less than three days, a trip that would normally have taken me a week or more, and it was still snowing. Fortunately, my heated grips and heated jacket were doing their job well, making the long days in the saddle bearable. A couple of the other riders were dismounting from their bikes at the end of a day's riding and looking utterly miserable. The dark horse of these high-mileage days was Tony, a middle-aged chap whose companion was a thirty-odd year old BMW. The bike performed admirably well in these early stages, averaging 80mph with the rest of the new bikes on the expedition, just occasionally demanding the odd roadside tinker to keep it from refusing to proceed.

The ferry crossing to Tangiers was rough. The Straits of Gibraltar are renowned for strong currents and high winds. Once in Tangiers, there were the formalities of customs to get through. We queued up in the two single-file lines, with armed guards on either side, and waited. The wait was prolonged. There were constant arguments between customs officers and the people wanting to gain access to North Africa. People hassled us from every angle, offering to 'help' us in our quest to continue on our adventure, offering to get us through the customs process with minimal fuss, just a handful of our hard-earned Euros in exchange. We declined. Instead, we waited patiently and took our turn in the queue. I amused myself by watching the cars trying to get in and out, being opened and searched by the officers, almost invariably finding contraband hidden in spare tyres, seats, boots, under bonnets, or in fact anywhere that wasn't immediately visible. This contraband would then be confiscated (unless money changed hands or other services were offered) and taken to the officer's shed. This process was repeated over and over, until the shed could take no more, then fewer cars were searched. It was bizarre. Eventually, after several hours of waiting in the cold and continuing snow, it was our turn. We were asked to hand over our passports, vehicle documents, some money (of course), and wait for the vehicles to be inspected if necessary. I had always been nervous of handing over my passport, and this incident was no exception. I had taken the precaution of photocopying all of my documents, and also carrying them on a memory stick in case all of the paper ones were lost or stolen. Much to my relief, after pawing over my documents and blowing the smoke of three crinkled cigarettes over them, they were handed back to their rightful owner. The officer gently licked the bottom edge of his curled moustache and asked me to help feed his children in this cold weather. I declined to make a 'donation' but thanked him profusely for allowing me entrance into Morocco, then headed out of the port to our agreed rendezvous point. By the time all the bikes were through customs it was dark. The process had taken much longer than anticipated, made worse in part by some members of the team not bringing their original documentation with them. At the meeting point, we checked our watches and opted for staying overnight in Morocco. Everyone was tired, most were cold, and we were all hungry.

The following day we awoke to sunshine. This was a novelty, and a most welcome one. The mood was high and infectious as we left the hotel, our saddles dry for the first time in days. We were to head towards the Atlas Mountains that day, with a tentative plan to stay overnight in a small motel high up in the hills. We were due to meet Ralph and his wife on their BMW at the motel; they had been touring through France and Spain prior to meeting the team. As we set off on the three hundred miles towards the mountains and started gaining altitude, the brief mood-lifting change in the weather deserted us and the heavy snows returned once more. Riding through more drifting frozen rain and ice, I was left wondering how many times Morocco sees snow, and guessed it couldn't be that often. The mountain passes were treacherous. Snow lay on the tarmac, the wind speed was 40mph or more in places, and most of the route was very exposed. On several tracks the wind was so strong that I had to angle the bike to thirty degrees just to keep it on a forward line. However, the little Suzuki continued to perform without complaint, achieving everything I asked of it. The buddy system had been well deployed with the remaining team members. The two Australian guys and girlfriend teamed up; Andy the army lad had teamed with another Andy, also on a Suzuki not dissimilar to mine; Geraint, the retired policeman from Wales, rode with Steve and me, and Tony pottered solo on his ancient BMW.

The final pass that we were due to ride through in the Atlas Mountains before making our overnight stop proved out of our reach. The snowfall over the previous few days had completely blocked the route, making any passage impossible, even by two wheels. Unfortunately, Ralph and his wife were on the other side of the pass, causing some headaches for Nick as to how we would all meet up. We were out of range for any phone network to be useful, so we had no way of reaching Ralph. Eventually, we decided that they would probably have found accommodation, and that the best we could do would be to retreat part way back down the mountain pass and find somewhere to stay for the night. After all, the snow showed absolutely no signs of letting up.

The expression 'beggars can't be choosers' has many applications, and it could aptly be applied to our accommodation that night. Miles from the next available bed, we stopped at a small eating-place with rooms available. In fact, none of the rooms in the place were taken, and the proprietor was utterly delighted that we had passed through. The Euros that this fortuitous stop would bring made his mouth visibly water and his left hand twitch slightly, as he turned on some lights for the outside hallway, showed us the outside toilet that the ten of us would share, then handed us keys to the rooms. If I'd had the option, I would rather have erected my tent and slept by the roadside. The rooms were littered with insects and animals in various stages of decay, seeming most happy to choose the shower floor as their last resting-place. I pulled back the bed cover to have a look, and was confronted by a multitude of bed mites and fleas, irritated at having their warm slumber disturbed. The light worked intermittently, only revealing new animal offerings when it did choose to function; the water was a deep brown and the heating had clearly broken. I elected to lay my sleeping bag on my rollaway mattress on the top of the bed without uncovering the insects inside, and Steve followed suit. We moved our already wet riding kit away from the leaking windows and out of reach of the drips of rain pounding the floor through the ceiling, then left for the 'restaurant'.

Steve and I decided to stick with tinned food, packets of biscuits and bottled drinks, while braver members of the team took up the offer of some cooked meat. It was difficult to tell when it arrived whether it truly was 'mountain hare', though the bones reminded me of those from a cat, which I remember from anatomy books of the distant past. Either way, some of the hot food found its way to the craving, expectant stomachs of the hungry riders. Interestingly, the proprietor sold out of tinned and packaged food early on that night, with most retiring hungry. 'Gotta put fuel in the furnace', I reminded the team, and advised that if any had bought packaged food, we should share it amongst us for nibbling overnight. This was a suggestion welcomed by most, and we duly shared the provisions around.

I was relieved at sunrise to only find six insect bites on my body, and remarked to Steve on my good fortune. He had not fared so well, having been bitten on most exposed parts of flesh during the night, resulting in an itchy rash that covered large areas of his body. I tended to the itching with some antihistamine tablets and cream, and we hastily packed our gear onto the bikes. I could not leave our host and his establishment quickly enough. It was easy to choose between remaining one second longer in the bug-ridden accommodation and riding off with wet clothes into the morning snow. We were heading south-west that day, hoping to meet up with our final team members the following night at the next arranged destination, four hundred miles away, south of Marrakesh, heading towards Agadir.

As we rode through the mountain passes and left the range, we took the opportunity to stop at the first reasonably sized village to eat and drink something recognisable and not insect-infested. We found a small fine hostelry serving kebabs and rice. The meat was fresh – the butchered animals were strewn across the front of the shop. Next door to the restaurant, a man hacked at a cow's head, desperate to remove the last strands of meat from the skull, while birds pecked and fought over the scraps of fat that hit the ground from his jabbing knife. We were all happy to feast on the freshly cooked meat, and drank pints of fresh sweet tea. An hour or so later, all riders mounted their bikes with a renewed enthusiasm not seen since Portsmouth. We had fed, rehydrated, the sun had finally come out again, and the skies had turned from grey to blue. At last, I felt the warmth of the morning sun on my clothes, and was amused as the water slowly evaporated from my sleeves in a steady drift of steam. 'Game on', I thought, 'Western Sahara here I come.'

Steve and I made steady progress with Geraint that day. We headed for Agadir, stopping only for petrol and occasional refreshment en route. I had decided that, whatever the proposed sleeping arrangement for that night, I would find a reasonable place to either pitch my tent or pay for a nice room. It was time, and Steve was jubilant at my suggestion. As it turned out, Agadir was fine. The hotel was comfortable – sure, I wouldn't have rushed back with Clare to spend an anniversary there, but it was warm, dry and almost insect-free, and for that we were all grateful. We had met up with Ralph and his wife on the way to Agadir, and it felt good to have the team complete.

The following day had us riding through Tiznit and on to the border between Morocco and The Western Sahara. Crossing the border was not dissimilar to entering Morocco, though less straightforward. Long waits at shanty huts signalled the exit from the relative civilisation of Morocco. The guard at the border had an inguinal hernia that was troubling him. I checked it out for him, which helped us get our papers signed in good time, though it didn't spare us from the need to make suitable 'donations' to various members of the customs team. As we left customs, we headed into 'no man's land', a ten-mile stretch of sand, rocks, abandoned cars, metal containers and rubbish that marks the border. This was the first taste of 'off-roading' for a couple of the team, and the bikes crashed with eye-watering frequency. I helped Steve up a couple of times until he'd gained the confidence to go a little faster. An increase in speed across the sand helps with the bike's control, whereas closing the throttle when deep sand is underneath just facilitates the front wheel sinking quickly and throwing the rider over the handlebars. There were a few locals hanging around this stretch to assist the rider in getting his vehicle unstuck, for a small fee.

Once in the Western Sahara, our passports needed stamping again, more donations were paid, and currency was purchased from one of several locals protected by a cluster of busy helpers eagerly trying to attract our business. With appropriate currency in our wallets, we headed off back onto tarmac, much to the relief of most of the riders. It was the sort of weather that most of us had expected from Africa – hot, dusty and dry. Hydration would now become a priority for us, as we rode through the small shanty villages of the Western Sahara. The satellite navigation systems were no longer of any use; maps and compass coupled with intuition became the standard means of orientation. The roads were mainly reasonable, just occasionally disappearing without warning to be replaced by crumbly old concrete, sand and dried mud. This meant concentrating hard at all times, otherwise the front wheel would leave the tarmac, fall into the sand and either throw the unwary biker swiftly from his machine or buckle the front wheel beyond repair. Steve and I kept an eye out for each other, and when either of us looked like we might be drifting into a tired, sleep-deprived state by driving erratically, the other would take to the front and we'd pull over for a brief rest, some water and a general chat about life. Our bikes continued to amaze the rest of the team, requiring nothing in the way of maintenance other than air in the tyres.

Our destination in the Western Sahara was Nouadhibou, situated on the border with Mauritania. With Algeria to the northeast and the Atlantic Ocean to the west, Western Sahara is a huge state, 103,000 square miles, and one of the most sparsely populated territories in the world. We rode through the largest city, Laayoune, home to over half the population of the territory, with about five hundred thousand inhabitants. Consisting mainly of desert flatlands, the riding was uninspiring. Dead and decaying animals littered the sides of the tarmac, dehydrated and disease-ridden. The rotting flesh provided homes for thousands of flies, only crawling out from the carcass when disturbed by the noise and vibration of a passing motorbike. The stench was stomach-turning, many roads smelling of death. It was a grim place. Aside from the rich phosphate deposits and fishing waters, the area has few natural resources and insufficient rainfall for most agricultural activities. Landmines laid throughout the territory both by the Polisario and the Moroccan army make straying from the 'road' a very foolish thing to do. Progress through the territory was relatively swift, all riders keen to press on to Mauritania in the hope of leaving the smell of death behind us.

On our final 'outward' day in Western Sahara, the team was first on the scene of a two-lorry collision. Carnage was rife, twisted metal and packed fish lay strewn across the tarmac, and two casualties lay by the side of the road. I stopped my bike and ran over to see what was happening, and attend to these two. The first had abdominal pain, a distended abdomen and various cuts and bruises, the second had a broken left upper arm and two broken legs. I splinted the broken limbs with what I could find by the roadside – some sticks and two strips of metal – administered some pain relief, and then tended to the first chap. He was unwell, probably suffering internal injuries, and drifting in and out of consciousness. We conversed for a while in pidgin French, enabling me to estimate the severity of his injuries. I thought he probably had a partially ruptured spleen and possibly liver as well. I intimated to one of the walking wounded that expedition of the ambulance, coming from a hundred miles or so away, was necessary. Eventually help arrived in the form of the police, and for once I wasn't asked to donate to their household funds. Instead, they assisted and agreed to stay until transport arrived. Finally we got the two casualties, still breathing, into the ambulance and on their way to a medical centre of some description. Working in the Accident and Emergency Unit at Whitby hospital had proved useful once again.

The first overnight stay in Western Sahara was an evening filled with excitement at the thought of leaving the extreme poverty and disease of the territory behind, and a lust to sample what Mauritania had to offer. We were soon brought back down to earth as we crossed the border, acknowledged our 'lack of appropriate paperwork' again, and made our donations to clothe and feed the police, and presumably to provide for their next gold teeth to join the mouthful they already possessed. I declined the invitation to give up my motorcycle gloves to one security man, as he desperately tried to convince me how cold he gets during the winter months in Western Africa on his moped. I explained that I had a greater need for them at present, and my other pair was being used by Jake, the rider on the KTM. Much to my sorrow, the roadside remained littered with old cow carcasses, occasional dead camels and dogs, only lessening as we approached a township. I thought about this for some time, and finally figured that the lack of dead animals near the towns suggested either that they could find nourishment there, or that the locals had shifted the bodies to thin out the stench that surrounded their homes. Either way, my nasal passages were glad of the relief.

Most towns that we rode through as we traversed Mauritania consisted of mud huts, corrugated iron sheds and street sellers. Invariably we would be brought to a standstill by the locals, mobbed for any 'cadeaux' that we might possess, and have to foil attempts to steal some part of our luggage. Nights were grim in Mauritania. We chose on occasion to camp in the desert rather than stay in towns, both for financial and safety reasons. I'd been largely guided by Nick's suggestion when choosing lodgings, except for our second night in Mauritania when, stinking from three days of desert sun, sweat and death, not having washed or eaten properly since Morocco, I decided to select a reasonable hotel before we crossed the border to Mali. Covering hundreds of miles a day is tiring, covering the distance on roads that are a mix of broken tarmac, sand, dirt and dust makes the level of concentration required that much greater. The constant stopping by security or police for roadside inspection of 'fiches' or documents, with the required bribery or fines also gets tiring. Arguing is not really an option, though bargaining is. Fines would often start at 100 Euros, and result in an amicable departure for 10 Euros or so. I can't really blame the locals for doing this, as we were obviously seen as the 'wealthy westerners', but the relentlessness of the situation irritated everyone.

Mauritania shares the same culture as that of Libya and Algeria, following Islam, with the majority of the citizens belonging to the Sunni sect. Encompassing 400,385 square miles, the territory is enormous, with more than three-quarters of it being made up of Sahara desert and the semi-arid Sahelian zone. The remaining portion lies along the Senegal River Valley in the extreme south and southeast. The climate is hot and dry, with frequent sandstorms, and the terrain consists of a plateau with huge sand dunes. It borders Senegal to the south, Mali to the southeast, Algeria to the northeast, with the Western Sahara to the north. People in the north follow a mainly nomadic lifestyle, whereas those in the south engage in some agriculture and livestock herding. The capital, Nouakchott, provided a civilised overnight stop to feed, wash and water ourselves. Steve and I picked a decent hotel for our night of luxury, and believe me the 50 Euros each was money well spent. As we met up with the rest of the team the following day, fresh from the dormitory-style hovel where they had spent the night defending themselves against a multitude of stinging insects and bugs, we knew we had made the correct choice. Sometimes, no matter how much travelling we do, a civilised night of clean sheets, decent food and rest is all that is needed to re-ignite the passion for the days ahead. It worked for Steve and I.

Mauritania is one of the least industrialised countries in the world. There is a fish processing plant and an oil refinery in Nouadhibou, a sugar refinery in Nouakchott and a meat-processing factory in Kaedi. Some production and partial processing of iron ore also takes place, and there is a textile factory in Rosso. It is clearly a country where people fear those in uniform, with the most common crimes being political murder, rape, theft and official corruption.

Our route from Nouakchott took us through Boutilimit, south of Kiffa, through Ayoun el 'Atrous, and south towards Mali. We elected to camp again prior to crossing from Mauritania into Mali, as townships were sparse.

The route to the desert camp had not been found without incident. Full of confidence, I'd ventured into the soft desert sand with a little too much excitement displayed through my right hand, the one that controls the throttle and hence my speed. As I buried my right foot in the sand to help the bike turn and avoid a rapidly-approaching tree, my foot caught on a rock and got trapped between a tree root and a large cluster of stone. I couldn't hold the weight of the bike, and, choosing between my leg and the bike, the bike unfortunately lost. I let go of the handlebars and spun awkwardly to the ground, watching helplessly as my motorcycle trotted on ahead of me, riderless. 'Snap!' I heard a gut-wrenching crack from the inside of my boot, and felt a warm rush 'wooosh' up my leg. 'Bugger me, that hurt!' I shouted inside my helmet. I sat, vacant, in the hot sand, wondering briefly what to do next. I gingerly removed my right boot, to reveal a puffed up, bruised and rapidly swelling ankle. 'Oh crap!' A stupid loss of concentration, and I was miles from any medical assistance. I hobbled up to where my bike lay, on its side, dumped in the sand where it had come to rest. She started up fine, and we both limped in to where the rest of the team had decided to set up camp. That evening, I fashioned a thin splinting system from an old piece of bandage and some crushed metal food tins – it would have to do. As long as I kept the bones reasonably well immobilised until I returned to the UK, then hopefully I would avoid too much permanent damage. Riding boots also afford reasonable protection to a fractured bone, and I trusted that the combination of my splint and the boot would work to achieve the intended aim, and hold the bones in place for the next nine thousand eight hundred miles. Once home, x-rays of the ankle revealed two fractures, already healed, with the bones reconnected fairly well.

Parking the bikes in a small clearing in the desert sand, we set up camp by early evening. A nomadic goat-herder passed by, thanking us for our offering of some water, and we settled into our tents. Sleep was disturbed twice that night, first by the discovery of an enormous spider, about ten inches across, which must have sneaked into my tent as I was erecting it. The second occasion was in the early hours of the morning, as the peace was shattered by a group of drunken locals driving round camp in a four-wheel drive. This latter disturbance could have had a nasty outcome, as I was well aware of the recent murders of tourists that had taken place just a few hundred miles away in Kiffa. Fortunately, after some screaming and shouting they left us alone. Our team decided to make a hasty exit from camp at first light, through fear of any repercussions. We did not want to find ourselves vastly outnumbered by angered, drunk locals in the desert under any circumstances. I had no sleep after the second disturbance, choosing instead to start packing up my equipment for the early departure.

The following day we crossed the border to Mali, and headed towards Bamako. With a population of nearly two million, Bamako is the capital and largest city of Mali. It is located on the River Niger, near the rapids that divide the Upper and Middle Niger Valleys in the southwest part of the country. It is the seventh largest West African urban centre and manufactures textiles, processed meat and metal goods, with commercial fishing on the river Niger. Temperatures in this region averaged around 32 degrees Celsius during our trip, and the approach to the city provided a welcome return to some reasonable tarmac roads. We'd been riding for twelve or more hours that day, and by the time we arrived at the outskirts of the city everyone was exhausted. Nick had arranged the overnight stay in an indoor 'camping-style' complex, consisting of mattresses on the floor, mosquito nets, showers, toilets and a place to buy food and drink. The journey through town to reach the hostel was a nightmare, fraught with difficult traffic, confusing directions and hot and humid conditions. Tempers were fraying as we circled endless roundabouts and lost Nick as he led the way to the hostel. After several altercations at the roadside between Nick and some members of the team, we eventually pulled into the overnight stopover towards midnight. It had been a long and difficult day. After some food and a beer, everyone retired for the night, having decided that the following day would be a rest day.

The next morning was spent in leisurely eating, rehydrating and tinkering with the motorbikes. Jake handed me back my winter gloves, as we were now experiencing temperatures in excess of 30 degrees daily, and set about trying to fix his KTM which had broken down yet again. The spare set of rear brake pads that I'd given him from my bike back in Morocco were working well, amazingly, as the fit was poor and we had had to change their configuration a fair amount to get them on. However, the problem was now electrical, and Brian, the other Australian, was a very competent mechanic who set about trying to help fix the problem. Steve and I had a brief check over our Suzukis, which were performing admirably, then wandered off for a look around town and to pick up some more tinned provisions. After supper, we went over the next stage of the route together, from Bamako to Segou, then San, heading east to Mopti, then finally Douentza, following the River Niger along the way. From Douentza to Timbuktu, the route was all off road. Considering the chosen bikes for our journey, some would clearly have more to be concerned about than others.

Heading out of Bamako was just as tiresome as heading in. We got lost going round the city several times, and eventually left the centre at mid-day, three hours after we set off, and in the most fearsome heat of the day. The plan had been to make Douentza in a day, but that just did not happen. The route was too long, and the roads too poor, necessitating a stop en route at Mopti. The stay turned out to be delightful, the hotel clean, the rooms cool and the food fine. Nick, Steve, Caroline and I ate together that night, telling stories and drinking wine. I got on well with Nick and Caroline, who were both good fun. Caroline and I had a career in common, Nick was eccentric, somewhat disorganised and laid back, with an infectious zest for adventure. We were to remain good friends after the trip. Nick discussed his plans to go with a group of motorcyclists from Ushiya in South America to Alaska, along the so-called 'Pan-American Highway'. The trip was huge, and I was certainly interested. However, the timing of the trip, March to May 2010, would potentially coincide with an adventure that I was planning. I was looking at trying a double-traverse of Mount Everest, summiting first by ascending the South route, over the top, then descending to North base camp. I would rest there for a day or two, then ascend the North route, over the top, then descend back to South base camp. It was an ambitious plan and would be the first time done if it was successful, and I was really keen to give it a go. I let Nick down gently, but suggested I may be interested in 2011.

We had made good time down this far, covering over six thousand miles in fourteen days. We left our haven in Mopti as a team once more, deciding to stay overnight in Douentza prior to tackling the arduous off-road section to our final destination. In Douentza we found a campsite that was truly sparse, but would serve as a base for our desert ride to Timbuktu. The showers were cold and the foot wells covered with insects of varying sizes, most of which I had never seen before. Steve and I got our tents sorted, ate some of our tinned food, and then set about changing his rear brake pads. He had also forgotten to bring spare ones, so I handed over my last spare set, as mine seemed in reasonable condition, and soon the job was done. Most of us were restless that night. The locals found the invasion of their township by the bikers an interesting phenomenon and naturally tried to extract some Euros from the group in various ways, but by morning all was quiet. We were swiftly out of our tents and ready for this final leg in the sand to our destination. All were excited, most were anxious, and a couple were frightened of what lay ahead.

The first few miles of the route were relatively straightforward: more dusty sand roads, the occasional blob of old tarmac and hard dirt, making riding fairly easy while standing high on the pegs. As we moved further into the Sahara, some members ran into trouble. After about twenty miles off road, I rounded some hard sand to find chaos in the soft sand beyond. Tony had come flying off his old BMW at some speed, his tank smashed and off the bike, along with various other parts of his machine. It looked like the trip was up for him, but he was unhurt. The bike was loaded into the back of Nick's truck, along with Andy the army lad's Honda, which had a broken rear suspension unit and a few broken plastics from hitting the sand at speed while trying to avoid Tony and his crashed bike. Eventually Steve and I continued down the track, which by now had turned into hard corrugations of dried mud interspersed with long stretches of deep soft sand. This was difficult riding, best negotiated at good speeds of 40-50 mph to avoid getting constantly stuck in the sand. Steve wasn't too confident about this, preferring to travel at 10mph and 'paddle' his way through the soft stuff. I sat on his tail all the way, helping him out when he fell off or his bike got stuck. He was clearly hating this section. After five hours in the intense heat of the Sahara, we reached the halfway point, designated by a village on the piste. It consisted of a few mud huts, and a place to shade and take a drink. After the brief stop, we climbed on to the scorching hot saddles again and pressed on.

It was imperative that we made Timbuktu by nightfall, as riding the route after dark would be extremely hazardous. Further down the track we caught up with Jake and his girlfriend, his KTM having broken down yet again. Any thoughts I'd ever had of buying one of these had now long disappeared. We sat with him for a while until Nick arrived to load yet another bike onto his now over-full truck. There was no room for any more bikes, so we were on our own now. After several falls avoiding donkeys resting in soft sand, misguided periods of false confidence, and stops to attend to pieces of motorcycle that shook themselves loose with increasing regularity, we finally reached the ferry to transport us across the Niger. Tarmac was waiting for us on the other side, signalling the end of a very tricky period in the saddle. Steve got down and kissed the ground, and we loaded our bikes onto the barge to take us across the river.

Just a few miles down the road on the other side of the river, we finally reached the mythical, mystical city of Timbuktu. I felt mightily relieved that the bike had got me there with virtually no trouble at all, vindicating my choice of machinery. Accepting an offer to be 'guided to where your friend is', we followed a young lad on his moped through the sandy streets of the city, eventually arriving at a small complex of tents and sheltered sleeping quarters where we were due to spend the night. Some of the other team members had arrived ahead of us and were enjoying a cold beer as daylight quickly faded to darkness; others were resting on their mattresses. We had just made the journey in daylight. Steve and I parked up the bikes and headed for a shower, before enjoying a well-earned meal of goat and potatoes washed down with some bottled water. We had arrived in Timbuktu, and what a journey it had been so far.

Some of the riders were keen to see if an alternative route existed for the return, instead of the off-road track back to Douentza. Unfortunately there was not, so some spent a restless night worrying about the rigours that lay ahead the following day. I woke early, and Steve and I breakfasted, then set off before the others. I was aware it had taken us nearly 13 hours to ride the dirt tracks, and wanted to be sure we made it in daylight. Before heading south back to the river and its crossing point, we took a little time to ride around the city. I wanted to pick up some trinkets for Steve and Lou's girls and some for friends and family, and get some photos taken. Timbuktu's lasting contribution to Islamic and world civilisation is scholarship. It is said to have one of the first universities in the world. By the 14th century, important books were written and copied in Timbuktu, establishing the city as the centre of a significant written tradition in Africa. The most outstanding treasures at Timbuktu are the hundred thousand manuscripts kept by families in the town. Some of these date from pre-Islamic times and the 12th century. The city was established by the nomadic Tuareg in the 10th century. Several Trans Saharan trade routes were established. Salt from Mediterranean Africa was traded with West African gold and ivory, along with large numbers of slaves. Mid way through the 11th century, new goldmines shifted the trade routes eastward, making Timbuktu a prosperous city where goods from camels were loaded onto boats on the Niger River. With a population of about thirty-two thousand, it is a UNESCO World Heritage Site, listed since 1988. If time had allowed, further exploration of this fascinating city would have doubtless been both enriching and extremely interesting.

As we headed back across the ferry, I said to Steve that I'd ride behind him all of the way to our campsite, and under no circumstances should we allow ourselves to be separated. He seemed grateful for this suggestion, as I was to his agreement; falling off or mechanical failure could prove disastrous without help. The journey back took a little less than ten hours, but entertained us with regular crashes, the usual bike issues, and livestock showing irritation at us intruding into their territory. Donkeys continued to block our path, and the areas of deep sand that we had avoided on the ride in we managed to find on the ride out. We arrived back in Douentza shortly before nightfall, tired, thirsty, and with sand in every penetrable crack. I was completely covered in sand, having ridden behind Steve all of the way back along the track, and the bikes were in need of a little fettling. However, the consensus was to pack up the gear left at the campsite the previous day and head straight on to the small haven we had found in Mopti, then rest there overnight and the next day. I must have fallen asleep a dozen times on the track to Mopti, just managing to wake myself up before falling off. I slept that night in my clothes, grateful at last to give my eyes and brain a rest from looking at the track in front. The following day, everyone rested, before the long, intimidating journey that lay ahead. I let my mind drift back to Clare and the dogs. I would have paid handsomely to step into my big bath at home right now with Clare, and see the little faces of Chino and Coco resting their heads on the side of the bath.

After our rest day, it was time to crack on with the journey home. Geraint joined Steve and me for most of the ride back, with Andy on the other Suzuki periodically riding with us too. The mood was generally upbeat. We all knew that home lay at the end of the road ahead, and that is a strong stimulant. As the days and nights passed, we made good progress back through Mali, Mauritania, Western Sahara and Morocco, and within a week or so we were back on the ferry to Algeciras. Nick's truck was still loaded with broken bikes, and Jake left us with the KTM, still working, to spend some more time in Morocco with his girlfriend. Once back in Spain, we spent one final night with the rest of the team in Malaga before heading up to Caen, covering fifteen-hundred miles or so in less than 48 hours to make the ferry. Such ridiculous distances I would never have dreamed possible prior to this trip, but now I know that they can be done. Steve, Andy and I parted company at the docks in Portsmouth, where unbelievably it was still snowing.

Six hours later, I was outside the shop that had helped me prepare the bike. Goose took a couple of pictures of the bike for the shop, chuckled at the state it was in, and I headed home where Clare was waiting for me. It had been an epic adventure, twelve thousand five hundred miles in twenty-seven days. My backside needed a rest from the saddle and the bike needed some sorting, but we had created some fantastic memories between us. Many friendships had been forged, some acquaintances tolerated, and the team had pulled together when needed.

Chapter 10
The Hardest Climb

Back home, I soon got to looking at plans for the double traverse over Everest. Clare and I spent some quality time together both at home and abroad, and once again the discussion of having a family came to the fore. Over the previous years, I'd not been that keen, there had just been too many expeditions that I had wanted to do, ambitions for places I'd wanted to see, and Clare had been ascending in her career, but now seemed like as good a time as any. We thought we'd remove any precautions, and see what happened.

We spent a lovely Christmas with our best friends Steve and Lou and their family. Their two dogs were delighted to have our two in their house, for it meant more food available for all concerned. January 2010 arrived, and we went on our annual pilgrimage to Lake Tahoe for some skiing and to see Clare's sister, Bernie. Each year we try to go to see Bernie and her husband Gil in San Francisco, and also my brother Andy and his family in New York. With the family so spread apart around the globe, keeping in touch becomes even more important.

Shortly after we got back from skiing, I fell over Chino, who was lying at the bottom of the stairs blocking access to the first step. As I fell, I cracked my head on the banister before landing heavily on the floor. Several minutes later, with a headache, I awoke being carefully nursed by both dogs. I must have been unconscious, but I seemed to have come to no harm so I just took myself off to bed. The following morning, I had developed some peculiar bruising down the left side of my neck, and my head was still aching. I plodded through the next few days at work until the discomfort subsided, and really thought nothing else of it, until two weeks later.

It was February 1st, 2010, a date etched in my mind forever. After a day off work, I'd spent the afternoon out running with Freda and the dogs, then retired to the bath for a good soak. As I was stepping into the bath, I felt an odd fast-creeping spasm over my lower neck. I stood up thinking I should go downstairs to get my phone. The neck pain moved swiftly to head pain and was disturbing my balance. I got my phone from downstairs and went back to my bed, just making it. I began to fear I was having a brain haemorrhage. To this day I have no idea why my thoughts were so accurate and clear, amidst the chaos that was taking place inside my skull. I lay on the bed, phoned Clare, who was on-call that evening in Scarborough, and explained what I thought was happening. Naturally horrified by this, she organised an emergency ambulance to come to the house, and phoned Toni, my brother-in-law and partner at our practice. He immediately set off for our house.

There was panic from the dogs, they knew I was ill. By this time, about an hour after the onset of the neck spasm, I could not move my head without deep, nauseating pain. My vision was affected, most things appearing hazy, and I thought I was going to die. After all, the majority of folk that suffer a brain haemorrhage do die, so I had every reason to fear my end was coming. I did my best to remain as calm as possible, as I knew that any movement or panic could result in extension of the bleed, but the pain was excruciating. I must have been verging on drifting into unconsciousness when the ambulance crew banged on the back door. The dogs, of course, went mad, after all the alpha-dog in the house, me, was sick, and they would do anything to protect me in this position. Chino, the softest dog in the world, was snarling and growling at the back door. Coco, as timid as ever, chose instead to lie with me, licking me profusely to try to make me better. Fortunately, Toni arrived – had he not done so, the ambulance crew would never have come in. Toni let the crew in, and took the dogs to the living room and closed the door on them. He then came upstairs to check me out, and looked visibly shocked to see my condition, and he put me on oxygen. It is preferable not to reduce the conscious level of someone in my unfortunate position too much, as it is important to monitor all neurological functions repeatedly to assess if the brain and its vital centres are becoming compromised by the blood and swelling in any way. The biggest risk of this type of haemorrhage, if death is not immediate, is increased swelling in the brain, or hydrocephalus. This can result in a condition known as coning, where the brain stem sinks down into the spinal cord. The result is death, and is rarely preventable.

We live at the top of a rough lane, and the winter had been particularly severe that year, the ambulance had not been able to gain access to our house. The ice up the lane lay thick on the road, and was coated over by fresh snowfall. Eventually, Toni and the paramedic got me to my feet, and helped me down the stairs. By now, I was vomiting with the pain, which made my head worse, as each retch raised the pressure inside my skull and caused the headache to worsen. It was an unpleasant spiral. Once outside the house, Toni walked me down to the bottom of the lane where the ambulance was waiting. The journey over to Scarborough Accident and Emergency Department was utterly miserable, every bump, every corner and every period of acceleration causing me to vomit, as my head pounded and my ears were filled with the 'whooshing' sound of my now sky-high blood pressure. I was sure, by now, that this was a brain haemorrhage. It fitted all the criteria. The outcomes were simple, survival, survival and suffer a stroke, survival and be incapacitated for ever more, or death. I had no idea which of the four categories would apply to me; it would largely depend on the cause of the haemorrhage, and the extent of the bleed in my brain.

Subarachnoid haemorrhages can be caused by several anomalies: bulges in a blood vessel that leak and burst; malformations in blood vessels that do the same, and true spontaneous haemorrhages – those where no obvious leaking blood vessel is found. On arrival into Scarborough, Clare rushed into the ambulance and held me tight. We were both very frightened. The man in charge of Accident and Emergency that night, James, had been one of my trainees at the practice. James is a good doctor and a very safe pair of hands, and I was glad he was there. The scan confirmed what I had feared, and it was a large, diffuse bleed. By this time Steve had arrived and asked me to pledge my motorcycles to him, jokingly of course, and wanted to know where the key to my safe was. Toni was still there, and was fantastic throughout. He had worked in Trauma and Accident and Emergency, and his help in the situation... well, I guess, I will never know what would have happened had he not been there. Clare was crying, her world falling apart before her eyes. Her forty-five year-old, fit husband, failing in front of her. Mike, one of the local GPs, was also on hand to offer help. Clare and I held each other desperately, unsure of how much longer we had together. The science was simple: if the blood vessel that had burst did not stop bleeding, then I would die.

Following the scan, I had to be transferred as quickly as possible to a main centre specialising in this type of disaster, in my case Hull Hospital. My memory of the journey is very sketchy. I was most likely drifting in and out of consciousness, for there were periods when the pain wasn't quite so intense. It is likely that these periods were when my brain was shutting down, preventing the sensory overload that took place when my consciousness was unaltered. Clare sat by my side in the ambulance, as we raced from village to village along icy roads, the sirens warning people periodically that time was of the essence.

Once at Hull, I was taken straight to the Intensive Care Ward. This would be my home for the foreseeable future. That first night was spent in and out of various scanners, as the consultants tried to determine the cause. It is very unusual not to find a cause with the size of bleed that I had, and if a cause was identified, then it would need treating to prevent further haemorrhaging. Every movement that I made, from moving a limb to trying to talk, resulted in the lining of my brain being stretched, and the series of pain spikes that it produced exhausted my body more and more. Morphine, codeine, anti-inflammatories were all given, though nothing made even a small dent in the relentless waves of vice-like tightening and throbbing that were taking place in my head. Clare held my hand tightly under the sheet. She had been told by the doctor in charge to say her goodbyes to me. He feared the worst and thought it unlikely that I would make it through till morning. It did not look good. I had spoken briefly to my father on Steve's phone when I was in Scarborough, telling him that I loved him and mum, and no matter what happened they had been the best parents that I could ever have wished for. I desperately wanted to speak with my brother and sister, but did not have the strength. I did not want to die, there were still too many things left that I wanted to do. Clare and I had many, many things left to do together, and I had not said goodbye to my dogs. It was all wrong, this was not in the script, this should not be happening. But it was, and nothing could change that fact.

During that first night, and the second, I had a recurring dream. I would feel pain as designated by a giant clock, and as the clock hand swept around the face and struck twelve, the pain came. The hand moved swiftly around the face, probably striking twelve every few seconds. But I was in a tunnel, or tube, which was not horizontal, but instead angled at varying degrees, depending on the pain that I was feeling. As I slipped down the tunnel, the pain lessened dramatically, so that near the bottom of it, I could hardly feel it. However, I knew somehow that pain was related to consciousness, and that consciousness was related to life, so I would scramble my way up this tube, against the gradient, so that I could be near the pain clock. This would strike twelve, assure me of the feeling of pain, thus reinforcing that I was conscious. Clare recalls me squeezing her hand with periodic tightening through the first twenty-four hours, this I imagine corresponded to the clock strikes. I knew that I must not let myself be seduced into drifting down the tube to the place where there was no pain, as I felt the relief at that point would be impossible to leave. It was like a see-saw inside the tube. The further I drifted down towards the pain-free end, the harder it would become for me to scramble back to the balance point. At the end where there was no pain, there was just a gradual tapering-off. The clock end, however, had a definitive 'stop' point. I was absolutely aware throughout, that if I got so far down the 'comfort' end, I would not be able to return to the conscious level. This unnerved me considerably, and became the overall focus of my first forty-eight hours in intensive care. There was no 'welcoming light' or open outstretched hands waiting to accept me at the comfort end of the tunnel, nor was there anything at the other end telling me that it wasn't my time. The interplay between me travelling to either end was complicated. It is a little difficult to describe in words. I was deep in the darkest and most frightening hours of my life.

During those first two days I remarked to Clare, in rare moments of lucidity, that Shep and Newman, our much loved dogs that had passed away several years previously, were sitting attentively by the side of my bed. It didn't seem at all strange that they were there, in fact, I remember taking a great deal of comfort from their presence. It was warming to see them both again, looking just as they had when they were in their prime of life. I find it perplexing now to fathom why I hadn't found their presence odd, but I drew strength from their reappearance, and vividly remember reaching out my left arm to offer them both affection as they waited patiently for me. My friend and colleague had also remarked, on one of the occasions that he visited me in hospital, that I had said

137

how good it was of them to let the dogs stay. He had thought that I was talking about Chino and Coco. Shep and Newman did not leave my side in those first few days in intensive care.

February 3rd brought slightly more clarity of thought and senses. Mother and father had arrived the previous day, along with Clare's twin brother Pete. Kevin, a long-time running companion had been ferrying people to and fro from the hospital most of the night, in true Kevin spirit. I vaguely remember seeing folk that day, but could not move in the bed choosing instead to lay in the foetal position and only move to perform bodily functions, even then as little as was absolutely necessary. I'd had another, more detailed scan, which had again proven inconclusive, but had shown a 'well developed foetal system of arteries'. Intermittent morphine provided a little respite from the persistent headaches, too strong to let me open my eyes as the light caused further irritation. I remember dad being tearful. We had always shared a really special relationship. He was my father, my mentor, and above all my friend. He'd only managed to keep himself sane in this crisis by befriending the bottle of Teachers whisky that we kept at the house for emergencies. Mother was the coping person in the relationship, always pragmatic in her outlook, and rarely fazed by situations, which was ideal, as dad needed her support at this time. Having them both there for Clare, along with Kevin, Toni and Pete, was of considerable comfort to me. Johnny Mac, another partner at our practice, had stepped up to the task almost immediately as well. I was lucky to have such friends and family around and, though I could not acknowledge it at the time, I was truly grateful for their help and support.

The early hours of day three were dark, for more reasons than one. I remember looking at the clock on the wall, it showed 02.25am. I had wanted daylight to arrive, as for some reason I felt less vulnerable during the day. Later I opened my eyes to look at the clock – or at least I thought I did. But I couldn't see the clock again, or anything else for that matter. I assumed that my eyelids were just stuck together with either the tears of pain or an early infection. I tried to prise them open with my thumbs and forefingers. It hurt. I had just put my fingers directly into both eyes – my eyes were already open, but I could not see. I lay back down, unsure what to do. I could not see – anything. It was utterly terrifying. I thought that was it; I had lost my sight forever. I presumed that there had been some spasm of the arteries that feed the eyes, and that, as these arteries are very small, maybe a blood clot had occurred in them. Either way, whatever had caused it, it was dreadful. 'Well, that's just fucking great!' I muttered to myself. 'How much more shit do I have to take?' I was angry and felt completely helpless. Over the next couple of hours, I started to plan my new life without sight. Could I ever work as a doctor again? I doubted it; I wouldn't be able to see what was wrong with my patients. I could never ride a motorbike again, obviously. God – I'd never see Clare or my dogs again, just feel them. I didn't call out for help, I didn't want any more help. I'd had enough of being poked around, I just lay still. For one very brief moment, I wished for a further haemorrhage, one that would finish this nightmare. But this made me even more angry. 'You selfish bastard!' I said to myself, 'you've just gone through a near-catastrophic medical disaster, and you are alive.' But it was hard. I lay still with my eyes shut, praying that when I next opened them, I would be able to see again. About four hours later, my prayers were answered. Clare had arrived to see me. She called my name from her seat beside the bed – I opened my eyes, and I could see her, all of her, and the rest of the room. I couldn't believe it. I felt tears coming down my cheeks, and Clare asked what was wrong. I didn't tell her, there was no need. But she looked so beautiful; she will never know just how lovely she looked to me.

Later on that day, I was able to sit up in bed, and think about eating some food. I'd been on intravenous fluids and injections for medication, but as the intensity and permanency of the headaches started to subside, I wanted to prove to myself that I was making progress. Up until then, my thoughts had been largely fixed around whether I could find a position, any position, in which the pain was not so intense. I had also briefly scared myself wondering if I would suffer any strokes in this 'post-haemorrhage' period. Strokes are common with this type of haemorrhage, and Clare knew that I would not have coped at all with losing the use of any limbs, or my sight. She had already spoken at length with the consultant in charge of my case, and explained that my pre-morbid life had been filled with activity. She had made the point that in the event of a cardiac arrest if it appeared that I would suffer severe brain damage I should not be resuscitated. We had spoken many times before about such things together, and she knew that I would have agreed with her a hundred per cent. It's a scary thought now, on reflection, but at the time this had been a real possibility. I had regained function and thought sufficiently to realise that this would now be my hardest climb. Still, whatever had been thrown at me before, I'd had some control over in terms of the eventual outcome. Somehow, in some way, I was determined that this would be no different, and that I could influence the final outcome of this disastrous event as well. I was determined to get better from this, no matter what it took, and enjoy some of the lifestyle of running, climbing and skiing that meant so much to me. It had to come right. It just had to.

The next few days were critical, both for the mental and physical improvement of the condition, and also for my friends and family to start seeing the return of my spirit. It remained intensely uncomfortable to move, cough or eat. A further series of scans of the blood supply to my brain and spinal cord circulation took place. I found myself walking a tightrope of expectation. On the one hand, I wanted them to find a reason for this haemorrhage, so that a further one could be prevented. On the other, I hoped that no cause would be found, as true spontaneous subarachnoid haemorrhages have the best prognosis if survived. No obvious cause was found, and by day eight I managed to get out of bed to walk to the toilet for the first time. Whilst the headaches remained, especially at night, they were improving. Following discussion with the consultant, it was obvious that I would be off work for at least six months, and that the headaches, general irritability, fatigue and inability to multi-task might persist for some time.

Interestingly, the Consultant remarked on the well-developed foetal circulation in my brain. My brain scans had all shown the same thing, and reported "a foetal-type posterior cerebral/communicating artery on the left hand side". This was an extremely unusual scenario, as this type of artery usually closes down or becomes redundant in a child after birth. It seemed likely that all of the high altitude climbing that I had done, spending time in low oxygen levels, had put sufficient stress on my brain for this circulation to re-open. It was likely that this saved my brain from more permanent damage. All of that pressure breathing, forcing my breath in and out of my lungs at high altitude, had reaped its reward, and had probably saved my life. Clare and I viewed it with differing meaning. I viewed this as a "green light" to continue climbing to high altitude, as surely I must keep this extra, well-developed circulation working, while Clare was slightly less optimistic about expeditions in the immediate future. Before the event, I had been blessed with a good memory, and had never had any problem undertaking two or three tasks at one time. Things were slightly different now. I had lost a bank of memory stretching back from January 2010, to August 2009, the reason for which remains unexplained but will probably be permanent. By day ten, I realised that undertaking more than one task at a time, such as watching the television and making a phone call, had become very difficult as the concentration required for one ruled out the other.

Recovery continued, and it was decided that I could leave hospital on day fourteen, providing I required no intramuscular medication overnight prior to discharge. That night was uncomfortable. I chose to decline injections in favour of tablets for fear of having to remain any longer in hospital. I felt ready to go home. I wanted to see Chino and Coco, lie next to Clare in our bed, and sit in the garden watching winter turn to spring. My parents and mother-in-law were waiting for me at home, having kindly offered to help out as Clare needed to return to work shortly after my return. My brother Andy had also flown over from the States to stay with me for a while, and as usual he was a real tonic. Over the previous few days, I'd been asking myself what I would be able to do now, whether I could still climb, whether I could still run, and whether I would retain the co-ordination to ride my motorcycle. I devised a rehabilitation programme for home, whereby I would start at week four walking 1 mile a day on the treadmill. Week five it would be increased to 2 miles a day, up to 5 miles a day from week eight. After this, I would try jogging 2 miles a day from week nine, then increase this by a mile a day per week up to 5 miles a day, after which I would try a long run of 10 miles or so. This programme became my fixation, and I did not allow myself any deviation from my schedule. If I could run again, then I could take whatever else life would throw at me. My running time would be thinking, relaxing, stress-relieving and rehabilitation all rolled into one. It would mean that we could run out with the dogs again, continue marathons, and remain fit for future climbs. All proceeded to plan, and by the sixth week, when I went to see the consultant, he was amazed at my progress. Physically I was improving daily, but mentally there were gremlins that I had to deal with. The headaches remained, still worse at night, causing fatigue. The concentration remained poor, the memory loss sustained, and the irritability noticeable. I have lost the vision in my right eye on two occasions, but the deficit has only lasted for about an hour then normal vision has returned, but other than that recovery proceeds well.

CLARE

It was a fairly typical Monday on call. I had operated on a patient with a perforated large bowel in the afternoon and had one more quick emergency case to do before I left the hospital to get home for dinner. Ali called me around seven in the evening and told me the spaghetti was ready and I assured him that I hoped to be home by eight. Twenty minutes later, my phone rang again and Ali's name came up on the screen. There had been a delay in getting the patient to the operating theatre and I was going to be late again! I answered the call and immediately started apologising. I often felt frustrated and guilty about the effect my job had on Ali and our home life. When Ali started to speak, I knew something was seriously wrong. His voice was different and some of his words were incoherent. He told me to call an ambulance as he had a severe headache. I asked him where he was and what had happened. He mumbled that he was lying on the bed but he was not able to say anything else. I hung up and the hospital switchboard put me straight through to the ambulance control centre. They asked me lots of questions about his condition, none of which I was able to answer but I told them I thought he was having a brain haemorrhage. They sent a team immediately.

When I put down the phone, I didn't know what to do next. Did I get in my car and drive the thirty minutes home, or did I stay in the hospital and wait for the ambulance to arrive. I knew the ambulance was stationed only a few miles from our home and that they would probably have left before I got there, but Ali was on his own. I called Ali again and he answered but he could only mutter a few sounds. I started to feel frightened. My brother-in-law, Toni, lived near us and I phoned to ask if he could go round to our house. Toni had just finished his clinic. I could tell he was tired and that he thought I was jumping to irrational conclusions, but I knew deep down that Ali was in trouble. He sighed, but agreed to go right round. Over the next ten minutes, I called Ali repeatedly until Toni answered the phone. Toni sounded shocked and told me that Ali was conscious but did not look well. They were going to bring him straight to A&E. The operating theatre sister on that night, Leslie, was standing beside me and she could see that something was wrong. I told her what I knew and she helped me to stay calm over the next few minutes. She made me a cup of tea, which went untouched, and called one of my surgical colleagues to cover my on-call.

In the meantime, I had called A&E and managed to get the CT radiologist and radiographer to come in, so there was no delay when Ali arrived. I also called our friends, Steve and Lou to tell them what was happening. Steve got straight in the car and came to the hospital. I then walked down the stairs to A&E to wait for him.

I watched while the paramedics wheeled Ali out of the ambulance and into the resuscitation room. His face was pale grey and sweaty and he was wrapped up in his favourite Ducati dressing gown. I still hate that dressing gown, although Ali continues to wear it. I gave him a cuddle, he squeezed my hand and I was bustled out of the way while the A&E doctor, James, got intra-venous access and did the initial assessment. They were just about ready in CT and I managed to get close to Ali again for a few minutes. I could tell he was in pain but they did not want to give him any analgesia until they knew what was going on in his head, in case it altered his level of consciousness. He kept his eyes closed most of the time but he opened them and told me that he thought he was going to die and that he loved me. I was fighting to stay calm to reassure him, and told him that I loved him and that he was going to be fine. When they took him to the scanner, I went outside to try and compose myself but couldn't help the tears falling.

I went back in and sat with Toni, Steve and Mike, another GP who was on call for the hospital. James came back and confirmed that Ali had suffered a sub-arachnoid haemorrhage or SAH. As part of my general surgical training, I had read much on the presentation and management of head injuries and I knew that the prognosis of SAH was not good. It all seemed completely unreal that this could be happening to Ali, the fittest and most health conscious person I knew. It felt like we were all stuck in some bad dream that we could not wake up from. Steve was the most focused at this time and he took Ali's phone to contact his parents, brother and sister. We were then allowed back in to see Ali while arrangements were made to transfer him to the nearest neurosurgical unit in Hull. I held him and stroked his head gently, feeling completely helpless and frustrated that he was still in so much pain. Ali asked for his phone and briefly spoke to his dad, telling him that he loved him. This really freaked me out and, as I did not want Ali to see me cry, I walked outside again for a few minutes.

The next forty-eight hours were the worst of my life. I did not leave Ali's bedside in the intensive care unit, except when he was taken away for the

MRI scan and angiogram. Ali rarely spoke but occasionally squeezed my hand. I wanted to climb into the bed beside him to hold him and comfort us both, but this is not what is done in hospitals. I felt completely alone, as my best friend and confidant was unable to help me through this crisis. He was too busy fighting for his life. The consultant informed me that Ali's angiogram did not show an aneurysm or abnormal dilatation of a blood vessel, which is the usual cause of a SAH and can be treated. In Ali's case, we could only sit tight and hope the bleeding stopped. Even if the bleeding did stop, Ali was at risk of further injury to his brain through the process of vasospasm. This is caused by the blood outside irritating the arteries, making them spasm and preventing the blood getting to the brain tissue. In a sense, this causes small strokes. He could lose the use of his limbs, vision or even speech and comprehension. I wanted Ali to survive, no matter what the final recovery would be. I knew, however, that Ali would rather die than live a life where he could not climb, run or function at a high level. He lived for the freedom and physical highs that climbing and running gave him. He would struggle to accept anything less.

We are lucky to live in a society where death in young people is rare and we all expect to live into our seventh decade. We never really dwell on death or have any real perception of our own frailty and mortality. Throughout all of Ali's adventures, I don't think I really believed that something bad would happen to him. Yet, here I was at thirty-seven years of age sitting in the intensive care unit, not knowing if my husband would survive a random brain haemorrhage, over which he had no control. I had a lot of time to think about this and found myself planning for all the potential outcomes, from a full recovery to death. I know this must sound morbid, but I think the mind tries to prepare itself for bad news and coping strategies kick in. My twin brother, Pete, came down on the first day. He saw Ali at his worst and took me away to the hospital canteen for a coffee. He told me that I had to prepare for the worst. I cried my heart out. During the night, as I sat by his bed, I prayed to God to let Ali live. I was brought up as a Catholic and, although I believe in God, religion had not played a part in my life for some time. Strangely, it did bring me some comfort in those long, dark hours.

Ali remained in terrible pain over the next week, with only small periods of relief when he was given morphine. It was hard to watch him suffer like that. He occasionally spoke to me, usually to ask me to get the nurse for pain medication. Although his condition had stabilised, I was still concerned *that he was going to die. In my years of being a doctor, I have found that patients are usually aware that they are going to die, even when they have been brought in with a sudden illness and have no prior medical knowledge. When Ali told me in A&E that Monday night that he was going to die, he truly believed it and so did I. This may sound strange, but Ali smelt different to me and seemed detached and distant. I think this was when he was in his tube. On the third day, he came back to me.*

As he improved, I was told I could only visit at the official visiting times, between 2-3pm and 7-8pm. I have worked in hospitals for many years, but being on the other side really opened my eyes to what the patients' and relatives' needs are. The most important person in your life is fighting for survival, but you have to conform to visiting times and crazy infection control policies that have little evidence-base and mean you cannot sit on the bed to comfort and touch your loved one. We have made huge advances in medicine and technology, but seem to have lost compassion along the way. I keep this in my mind at all times now and I hope this has made me a better doctor.

Ali tackled his recovery just like one of his climbs. He pestered his consultant to agree to a rehabilitation schedule, which I felt was too ambitious but was typical of Ali. He has surprised everyone and, apart from some minor memory issues and headaches, he is back to normal. We had a huge amount of support from our family, friends and colleagues and I owe many such a debt of gratitude that I will never be able to repay. The last seventeen years with Ali has been a journey for us both, with magnificent summits and occasional deep crevasses to overcome. The complexities and obligations of daily life often take priority over relationships and we fail to devote time to our loved ones. It is not until you come close to losing something that you truly appreciate its value. Ali is priceless!

It's now six months since the haemorrhage, and I run every day. The dogs love having me at home and love the morning runs with Freda, Paul, Clare and me. Freda and I were supposed to have run the London Marathon together again in April 2010. This would have been my 50th marathon but unfortunately circumstances dictated otherwise. However, we are back training as a team now, something I could have only dreamt about back in February 2010, and for that I am truly thankful. The motorbike has been dusted off, in the expectation of another trip to the Isle of Man TT races. Clare is back to working full-time, and I go to my practice meetings every week to keep myself up to speed with developments. Hopefully I will return to work in a few weeks or so, on a part-time basis initially, under the very helpful guidance of the Occupational Health Consultant. I'm keen to return, as, having never had a day off through illness in nineteen years, this has come as a shock to my system. My biggest fear at present is that I shall not be able to undertake all the tasks required to be a successful and safe General Practitioner again, but this will only be tested by getting in there and doing the job. With the help of the partners at work, all of whom have been very supportive, and an excellent Practice Manager, I shall soon be pondering through the medical conundrums of life and my patients once more.

What lies ahead for me and Clare? Maybe we will have a family. Having had discussions with the consultants who were overseeing my care, I am reassured that there is no suggestion that the brain haemorrhage will recur, and that there is no medical reason why I should not return to the environments that I love so dearly. After all, overcoming challenges is what empowers us to understand what we are capable of, and climbing high mountains presents me with the right environment to look deep inside myself. None of us really has any idea what may lie ahead. The important thing is to embrace each moment for what it is, live it, then continue forward, for it will never return. We are all put to the test, but it never comes at the point or in the form that we would prefer.

As the dust on the emotional and physical trauma settles, the need to talk about a life-threatening, catastrophic medical disaster becomes greater than any individual's ability to listen. That is the time to move on, to try, as far as possible, to put events in the past, where they should remain. Why did I survive the brain haemorrhage without any residual medical problems? Why did it happen when I was in the safety of my own home, in my own country, and not in a tent up a mountain in the middle of nowhere, and why did it happen to me at all? I will never have the answers to these questions.

Two things, however, I am now certain of. Because of my experiences during the time immediately after the brain haemorrhage, I am sure that when we die, or as we get close to it, we feel no pain. Secondly, I am confident that when we die we are alone. Even though Clare and I were physically together as I drifted towards and away out of 'place with no pain,' and even though I was intermittently aware that she was around, my battle for life was so intense that I was sharing space and time with no-one else. I was in my own sphere – a dimension in which no other being existed. Clare held me tight, but she had never felt more alone; I gave no input to try to alleviate the pain and sorrow that she was experiencing. We were together, but in separate places.

And now, of course, the maps and equipment have once again made their trip out of storage and into the spare room, as plans for the traverse of Mount Everest once again get under way.

'Never, ever, ever give up.'
Sir Winston Churchill

'You only fail if you quit.'
Lance Armstrong

'What lies before us and what lies behind us
is tiny to what lies within us.'
Ralph Waldo Emerson

Acknowledgments

I owe thanks to many people for the events that have taken place in this book. To my brother Andy and sister Lara for their humour and support through my life thus far, and to Clare's family, especially Peggy and Bill, for embracing me into their family and supporting Clare during my frequent absences. I would like to thank all those at Whitby Group Practice for their encouragement, and for covering my work during these adventures, and, of course, to my patients for their support and interest too. To Steve and Lou Johnson for always being there for us, and to their daughters Cas and Hel for making us smile over the years. A special thank you is extended to Sir Chris Bonington, who has been a fantastic inspiration to me, and to Alpine Ascents, International Mountain Guides and Jagged Globe for helping me realise my dreams. I also extend my thanks to St Catherine's Hospice, for providing me with a most worthy purpose for my fundraising efforts, and the community of Whitby and the surrounding areas for their relentless support in donating to this great charity, and also to Paul and Steve for casting a critical eye over the manuscript.

I'd like to thank Kevin Duffy at Bluemoose Books for his help in getting my manuscript to the public, and also the Bluemoose editorial team; Hetha Duffy, Leonora Rustamova and Lin Webb.

But finally, and most importantly, I'd like to thank my lovely wife Clare for her complete devotion, affection and constant belief in me, and my mum and dad, Janet and Norman Sutcliffe, for their tolerance, love and continual encouragement that only a parent can give to their offspring. None of this would have been possible without you, and I thank you from deep within my soul.